DOCTOR JOHNSON
AND OTHERS

BY

S. C. ROBERTS

*Master of Pembroke College
Cambridge*

OCTAGON BOOKS

A DIVISION OF FARRAR, STRAUS AND GIROUX

New York   1976

© Copyright 1958
by
Cambridge University Press

Reprinted 1976
by special arrangement with Cambridge University Press

OCTAGON BOOKS
A DIVISION OF FARRAR, STRAUS & GIROUX, INC.
19 Union Square West
New York, N.Y. 10003

Library of Congress Cataloging in Publication Data

Roberts, Sydney Castle, Sir, 1887-1966.
   Doctor Johnson, and others.

   Reprint of the ed. published by Cambridge University Press, Cambridge.
   1. Johnson, Samuel, 1709-1784. 2. English literature—History and criticism—Addresses, essays, lectures. 3. Authors, English—Biography. I. Title.

PR3533.R543   1976   828'.6'09   76-46507
ISBN 0-374-96847-0

Manufactured by Braun-Brumfield, Inc.
Ann Arbor, Michigan
Printed in the United States of America

CONTENTS

Preface		*page* vii
I	THOMAS FULLER	1
II	PEPYS AND BOSWELL	24
III	DOCTOR JOHNSON	40
	1. The Moralist	40
	2. The Churchman	69
	3. The Biographer	81
	4. Dr Johnson and the Fairies	99
IV	THOMAS GRAY OF PEMBROKE	106
V	TWO CLERGYMEN	131
	1. James Beresford	131
	2. Benjamin Wrigglesworth Beatson	147
VI	MAX BEERBOHM	156

PREFACE

Thomas Fuller claimed that no stationer had ever lost by him. I, on the other hand, am keenly aware that a collection of essays and addresses tends to feed an author's pride rather than a publisher's pocket.

Consequently, I am even more than usually grateful to the Syndics of the Press for undertaking this book; I am also indebted to the following for leave to reprint: the Manchester University Press ('Thomas Fuller'); the British Academy and the Oxford University Press ('Dr Johnson the Moralist'); the editor of *The Church Quarterly Review* ('Dr Johnson the Churchman'); Messrs. Faber & Faber ('Dr Johnson and the Fairies'); Messrs. Jackson, Son & Co., publishers to the University of Glasgow ('Thomas Gray of Pembroke'); also to Yale University for the extracts from Boswell's diary.

I cannot claim any formal unity for the book save, perhaps, that all the essays spring from a love of the biographical part of literature.

S. C. R.

November, 1957

I. THOMAS FULLER[1]

The history of the literary work and reputation of Thomas Fuller is a curious one. Between 1639, the year of the publication of *The Holy War*, and 1661, the year of his death, he successfully published more than thirty books, some of them quite slight, but five of them contained in very substantial folios.

For 150 years after his death he was decried or neglected. Then, suddenly, he was re-discovered by Southey and Lamb and Coleridge. Writing in 1811, Lamb noted that Fuller's works were 'scarcely perused but by antiquaries' and accordingly he collected 'some specimens of his manner, in single thoughts and phrases' for the benefit of the general reader, thereby setting an example which many anthologists were to follow. To Lamb, indeed, Fuller's works were 'books of the true sort, not those things in boards that moderns mistake for books' and he was troubled with severe eye-strain with 'reading thro' three folios of old Fuller in almost as few days'. Coleridge was even more extravagant in his praise: 'Next to Shakespeare, I am not certain whether Thomas Fuller, beyond all other writers, does not excite in me the sense and emotion of the marvellous'; and again: 'Shakespeare! Milton! Fuller! De Foe! Hogarth! As to the remaining mighty host of our great men, other countries have produced something like them—but these are uniques.'

This romantic adulation had its due effect. In the nineteenth century all of Fuller's major works and many of his

[1] The Ludwig Mond Lecture, Manchester, 1953.

minor works were reprinted and these new editions were supplemented by a biography planned on an encyclopædic scale.

At the beginning of the present century came the inevitable reaction. Critics began to refer to Fuller as 'the spoilt child of criticism' and as a writer whose 'very faults' were found 'charming in the eyes of his doting admirers'. Historians of seventeenth-century life and literature either disregarded his writings entirely or dismissed them in a curt phrase. 'Eminently readable, if never profound', writes a Scotch critic, and a French savant refers, in a footnote, to Fuller's 'usual blemishes of bad taste and misapplied wit'.

Two results have followed: first, Fuller's writings are for the most part unknown to the generality of readers; secondly, such knowledge as there is of them is derived from little books of extracts.

The wit and wisdom of Thomas Fuller—Pulpit sparks, being XIX Sermons of that godly and popular Divine Thomas Fuller—Wise words and quaint counsels of Thomas Fuller—Quaint thoughts of an old-time army chaplain—Quaint Nuggets; such are the titles of some of the anthologies published in the last century. Fuller, in short, is so attractively quotable in snippets that few are in danger of the eye-strain which the reading of his folios induced in Charles Lamb.

'Sir,' said Dr Johnson, 'the biographical part of literature is what I love most' and for a proper appraisal of Fuller's achievement it may be well to survey briefly the course of his comparatively short life.

Thomas Fuller was born at Aldwincle in Northamptonshire in 1608. His father, of the same name, was

Rector of the parish, had been a Fellow of Trinity College, Cambridge, and was married to the sister of John Davenant, Bishop of Salisbury, who had been Lady Margaret's Professor of Divinity and President of Queens' College until 1621. Accordingly, the young Fuller was sent up to Queens' at the early age of thirteen. In 1628 he proceeded to the degree of M.A. and had the distinction of being the youngest Master of Arts in the University. In spite of his uncle's commendation, he was not elected to a fellowship and so migrated to Sidney Sussex as a fellow-commoner. In 1630 he was ordained and presented to the curacy of St Benet's Church, which he held for about three years. His oldest parishioner was Thomas Hobson, whose funeral service he conducted. Fuller was now twenty-two years of age and he quickly embarked upon the main occupations of his life—preaching and writing. His first book, a poem entitled *David's Hainous Sinne*, was published in 1631, but even his most ecstatic admirers have never acclaimed him as a poet. In the same year his uncle, the Bishop of Salisbury, secured for him a prebend in the Cathedral and three years later presented him to the rectory of Broadwindsor in Dorset. Here he was able to pursue the line of antiquarian study that most appealed to him and in 1635 he duly fulfilled the exercises required for the degree of Bachelor of Divinity at Cambridge. In 1638 he married Ellen Grove, daughter of William Grove, M.P., and in 1639 his first important book, *The Historie of the Holy Warre*, was printed at the University Press at Cambridge. With the success of this book Fuller had good cause to be pleased; by 1651 it had reached its fifth edition. In his address to the Reader, Fuller was perfectly frank. He did not boast of original research. The materials, he said, were found to his hand; he acknowledged most of his authorities in the margin and made a list of them at the end of the book. In his dedicatory epistle to the Hon. Edward Montagu and the Hon. Sir John Powlet, he reveals his own view of history:

> Now know, next Religion, there is nothing accomplisheth a man more than Learning.... If you fear to hurt your tender hands with thornie School questions, there is no danger in meddling with Historie, which is a velvet-study and recreation-work.... Historie maketh a young man to be old, without either wrinkles or gray hairs; priviledging him with the experience of age, without either the infirmities or inconveniences thereof. Yea, it not onely maketh things past, present; but inableth one to make a rationall conjecture of things to come. For this world affordeth no new accidents, but in the same sense wherein we call it *a new Moon*, which is the old one in another shape....

Thus quickly does Fuller pass from his somewhat naïve definition of history to one of the fundamental problems which still exercise the historian.

Fuller's election in 1640 as Proctor in Convocation for the diocese of Bristol may well have been prompted by the success of *The Holy Warre*. In London he acquired popularity as a preacher and his first book of sermons (*Joseph's Party-Coloured Coat*) belongs to the same year. In the following year his wife died after giving birth to a son and Fuller left Broadwindsor for good. Moving to London, he first preached at the Inns of Court and was soon afterwards appointed Preacher at the Chapel Royal, Savoy. Meanwhile, the political storm was gathering. The Long Parliament had met in November 1640 and during his two years at the Savoy Chapel Fuller endeavoured to preach peace. His own sentiments were as clearly Royalist as they were anti-Papist and he strove hard for a *via media*. 'The best and onely way', he said, 'to purge errors out, is in a faire and peaceable way; for the sword cannot discerne betwixt truth and errour; it may have two edges, but hath never an eye'. In his last Savoy sermon (27 July 1643) he declared:

> O the miserable condition of our Land at this time! God hath shewed the whole world that *England* hath enough in it selfe to make itselfe happy or unhappy, as it useth or abuseth it. Her homebread wares enough to maintain her, and her homebred warres enough to destroy her, though no forreigne Nation contribute to her Overthrow. Well, whilest others fight for Peace, let us pray for Peace; for Peace on good termes, yea, on Gods termes and in Gods time, when he shall be pleased to give it, and we fitted to receive it. Let us wish both King and Parliament so well as to wish neither of them better, but both of them best. Even a happy accommodation.

But the accommodation was not reached and Fuller was compelled, with others, to take refuge in Lincoln College, Oxford, being distressed especially by the loss of part of his library. Meanwhile *The Holy State and the Profane State* had been printed at Cambridge in 1642 and it is not the least remarkable feature of Fuller's literary career that his most popular book should have been written during the *sturm und drang* of war's alarms.

In May 1644 he preached a notable sermon before the King in St Mary's Church, but by this time he had been attached to Sir Ralph Hopton as an army chaplain and had lived through the siege of the Basing House. From Oxford he went with the Royalist army to Exeter and there he produced his *Good Thoughts in Bad Times*, published in 1645. Both the title and the content of the little book were characteristic. Always he longs to bring the contending parties together:

> In Merionethshire in Wales, there be many mountains whose hanging tops come so close together, that shepherds, sitting on several Mountains may audibly discourse one with another. And yet they must go many Miles, before their Bodies can meet together, by reason of the vast hollow Valleys which are betwixt them. Our Sovereign and the Members of his Parliament at London seem very near agreed in their general and publick Professions. Both are for the Protestant Religion; Can they draw nearer? Both are for the Privileges of Parliament; Can they come closer? Both are for the Liberty of the Subject; Can they meet evener? And yet, alas, there is a great Gulf, and vast distance betwixt them, which our sins have made, and God grant that our Sorrow may seasonably make it up again.

But not all Fuller's meditations were upon the state of the nation. Sometimes, with unaffected and disarming candour, he would reflect upon his own weaknesses:

> I discover an arrant Laziness in my soul. For when I am to read a Chapter in the Bible; before I begin, I look where it endeth. And if it endeth not on the same side, I cannot keep my hands from turning over the leaf, to measure the length thereof on the other side; If it swells to many verses, I begin to grudge. Surely my heart is not rightly affected. Were I truly hungry after heavenly Food, I would not complain of Meat. Scourge, Lord, this laziness of my Soul, make the reading of thy Word, not a penance but a pleasure unto me, teach me that as amongst many heaps of Gold, all being pure, that is the best, which is the biggest, so I may esteem that Chapter in thy Word the best, which is the longest.

In this and similar passages we are carried forward in spirit to the limpid candour which we associate with Samuel Pepys and James Boswell.

At Exeter a daughter was born to the Queen. Fuller was appointed chaplain to the infant Princess, and duly presented her with a copy of *Good Thoughts in Bad Times*. For the publication of his more substantial work, the *Church History*, the times were naturally unpropitious. 'For the first five years during our actual civil wars,' he wrote, 'I had little list or leisure to write, fearing to make a history, and shifting daily for my safety. All that time I could not live to study, but did only study to live.' Nevertheless, he characteristically made use of such opportunities as he had. Besides the *Church History*, he had in mind his work on the *Worthies of England* and in the course both of his wanderings with Hopton's army and of his sojourn at Exeter he spent what time he could in investigating local antiquities.

Nor did the good doctor ever refuse [says his first biographer] to light his candle in investigating truth from the meanest persons' discovery. He would endure contentedly an hour's or more impertinence from any aged church-officer, or other superannuated people, for the gleaning of two lines to his purpose.

When Exeter fell to the Parliamentarian forces in 1646, Fuller made his way back to London. Life was not easy for him. He failed to 'be restored to the exercise of his profession on terms consisting with his conscience', but he had good friends. His publisher, John Williams, first took him under his roof and later Edward, Lord Montagu, who had been with him at Sidney Sussex College as a fellow-commoner, gave him hospitality at Boughton House in Northamptonshire. Here he wrote *The Cause and Cure of a Wounded Conscience*. This was published in 1647 and was shortly followed by *Good*

Thoughts in Worse Times, which became a very popular manual. In 1649 Fuller was presented to the perpetual curacy of Waltham Abbey by Lord Carlisle, an appointment which greatly facilitated his literary work. He made good use of Sion College Library and Lord Middlesex put the books at Copt Hall at his disposal. His *Pisgah Sight of Palestine*, an elaborately illustrated and exhaustive account of the Holy Land, was published in 1650 and won high praise from contemporary scholars. In the following year Fuller married a second wife (Mary, daughter of Lord Baltinglass) and for the next few years was busy in writing, and publishing, lectures and sermons. In 1655 he at length completed his *Church History of Britain*, to which was appended a *History of the University of Cambridge* and a *History of Waltham Abbey*. This was his *magnum opus*. It was the first time that such a work had been attempted since the days of the Venerable Bede and even those who are critical of Fuller's general style and treatment have paid tribute to the *Church History* as a monument of industry, research and courage. Shortly before its completion a friend twitted Fuller with the remark that if he did not hasten his work, the 'Church of England would be ended before the History thereof'.

Blessed be God [wrote Fuller in his preface] the Church of England is still (and long may it be) in being, though disturb'd, distempered, distracted. God help and heal her most sad condition. The three first Books of this Volume were for the main written in the reign of the late King. The other nine Books were made since Monarchy was turned into a State.

In 1658 Fuller was presented to the rectory of Cranford, in Middlesex, by Lord Berkeley and in the following year had to face the *Examen Historicum* of Peter Heylin, who claimed to have found 350 mistakes in the *Church History*. Fuller, of course, was ready with his reply, which he entitled *The Appeal of Injured Innocence*. Unlike most controversialists, however, he appended a letter to his adversary with proposals for an amicable agreement, and eventually the two men met in a friendly interview which is said to have led to a 'perfect amiable closure and mutual endearment'.

In the early months of 1660 Fuller was again busy with his pen and his *Mixt Contemplations for Better Times* were dedicated to Lady Monck. At the Restoration he recovered his living at Broadwindsor, his preachership of the Savoy and his prebendal stall at Salisbury; he was also made a D.D. by royal mandate and appointed Chaplain Extraordinary to the King. Had he lived, he would doubtless have been a bishop, but he died of typhoid fever in August 1661 and was buried in the church at Cranford. He left behind him a truly great work, *The History of the Worthies of England*, part of which was already printed at the time of his death. It was published by his son, John, in 1662 and is the crowning monument of Fuller's remarkable fertility of research and exposition. Singlehanded and in a single work he had set out to provide what we now look for in the *Victoria County History* and the *Dictionary of National Biography*.

Even the briefest outline of Fuller's life and work is enough to show his readiness to embark upon vast areas of study from which the modern specialist would select one small portion for intensive treatment:

I know the generall cavill against generall learning is this, that *aliquis in omnibus est nullus in singulis*. He that sips of many arts, drinks of none. However we must know, that all learning, which is but one grand Science, hath so homogeneall a body, that the parts thereof do with a mutuall service relate to, and communicate strength and lustre each to other.

This is taken from *The Holy State* and, since Saintsbury rightly remarks that no one should think he understands Fuller until he has at least read one of his books *in toto*, it may be well to consider *The Holy State* as something more than a mine of amusing quotations.

The work is divided into five books, of which the last deals with *The Profane State*. Of the first four, Book I deals with domestic types—the Good Wife, the Good Husband, the Elder Brother, the Constant Virgin...; Book II with occupations and professions—the Good Physician, the True Church Antiquary, the Controversiall Divine, the Good Master of a Colledge...; Book III contains what Fuller calls General Rules on such subjects as Hospitality, Anger, Moderation, Marriage...; and Book IV treats of public figures—the Wise Statesman, the Good Bishop, the True Nobleman, the Ambassador, the King. Book V, as its title suggests, exposes the vices of the Harlot, the Heretick, the Traitour, the Tyrant and other evil-doers.

For most of his ideal types, Fuller supplies a suitable example from biblical, ecclesiastical, or secular history; thus Abraham exemplifies the Good Husband, St Hildegard the Constant Virgin and Lord Burleigh the Wise Statesman.

The Holy State offers the reader a wide variety of instruction and entertainment and from the purely literary point of view may be studied in its relation to the early development of the English essay, to the many Character-writings of the period, to the courtesy-book and to the nascent art of biography.

Fuller's reading was wide and much careful analysis has been made in recent years of his indebtedness to Thomas Heywood, to Nicholas Breton, to many character-writers and, in particular, to Francis Bacon. To the historians and critics of literature such borrowings are of real interest and importance; but just as it is possible to enjoy Shakespeare's plays without full knowledge of the sources of his plots, so may Fuller's text be read and appreciated without deep inquiry into the writers who influenced him. What Johnson said of Pope—'he wrote for his own age and his own nation'—is, of course, peculiarly true of Fuller: in the troubled times in which he lived, he was personally and intimately involved in matters of civil and ecclesiastical policy and many of the characters which he draws have the full flavour of the seventeenth century. In his sketch of *The Faithfull Minister*, for instance, there is a noteworthy emphasis upon the importance of good preaching: 'He will not offer to God of that which costs him nothing; but takes pains aforehand for his Sermons.... Having brought his Sermon into his head, he labours to bring it into his heart, before he preaches it to his people.' Admirable, but perhaps slightly conventional, advice to a young clergyman; but Fuller's elaboration of his point is characteristic:

> Surely that preaching which comes from the soul most works on the soul. Some have questioned ventriloquie, when men strangely speak out of their bellies, whether it can be done lawfully or no; might I coin the word *cordiloquie*, when men draw the doctrines out of their hearts, sure all would count this lawfull and commendable.

For an example of the faithful minister Fuller chooses William Perkins, the 'learned, pious, and painfull Preacher of God's word at St Andrew's in Cambridge':

After his entrance into the Ministry the first beam he sent forth shewed to those *which sat in darknesse and the shadow of death*, I mean the prisoners in the castle of Cambridge.... Perkins prevailed so farre with their jaylour, that the prisoners were brought (fetter'd) to the Shire-house hard by, where he preached unto them every Lords day.... His sermons were not so plain but that the piously learned did admire them, nor so learned but that the plain did understand them.... He would pronounce the word *Damne* with such emphasis as left a dolefull Echo in his auditours ears a good while after. And when Catechist of Christ-College, in expounding the Commandments, applied them so home, able almost to make his hearers hearts fall down, and hairs to stand upright.

From this sombre spectacle of terrified undergraduates I turn with lively expectation and some apprehension to the description of 'The good Master of a Colledge'. It opens with a general warning and a parallel wholly typical of Fuller's utilisation of his historical reading:

The Jews *Anno* 1348 were banished out of most countreys of Christendome, principally for poysoning of springs and fountains.' Grievous therefore is their offense, who infect Colledges, the fountains of learning and religion; and it concerneth the Church and State, that the Heads of such houses be rightly qualified....

Then with a relevance not confined to the seventeenth century, follows the first Maxim:

His learning if beneath eminency is farre above contempt. Sometimes ordinary scholars make extraordinary good Masters. Every one who can play well on Apollo's harp cannot skilfully drive his chariot, there being a peculiar mystery of Government. Yea as a little allay makes gold to work the better, so (perchance) some dulnesse in a man makes him fitter to manage secular affairs; and those who have climbed up Parnassus but half way better behold worldly businesse (as lying low and nearer to their sight) then such as have climbed up to the top of the mount.

Yes, the dons have a word for it, a word familiar to all who serve on academic councils. Compared with Fuller's picturesque vignette, how flat and colourless it sounds—the Good Administrator.

In his chapter *Of Books*, Fuller begins conventionally with the inevitable quotation from *Ecclesiastes*, but his maxims are shrewd enough: 'It is a vanity to persuade the world one hath much learning by getting a great library.... Few books well selected are best.'

Fuller in fact was a reader rather than a bibliographer and deprecated 'the vain humour of many men in gathering of Books'. Furthermore he knew that not all books are to be read from cover to cover.

Some Books [he writes] are onely cursorily to be tasted of. Namely first Voluminous Books, the task of a mans life to reade them over; secondly, Auxiliary Books, onely to be repair'd to on occasions; thirdly, such as are mere pieces of Formality, so that if you look on them you look thorow them; and he that peeps thorow the casement of the Index sees as much as if he were in the house.

But there were some books that deserved much more:

The lazinesse of those cannot be excused who perfunctorily passe over Authours of consequence and onely trade in their Tables and Contents. These like City-Cheaters having gotten the names of all countrey Gentlemen, make silly people believe they have long lived in those places where they never were, and flourish with skill in those Authors they never seriously studied.

Fuller appreciated something of the economics of book production and once claimed that no stationer had ever lost by him. *The Holy State* was printed at the University Press, where Fuller's remark that 'Learning hath gained most by those books by which the Printers have lost' was no doubt fully endorsed.

One of Fuller's chapters is entitled *Of Tombes*. No subject evoked the organ-tones of seventeenth-century prose with greater splendour than that of mortality. Who can forget the solemn warning of Sir Thomas Browne:

> The iniquity of oblivion blindly scattereth her Poppy, and deals with the memory of Men without distinction to merit of perpetuity.... Since the Brother of death daily haunts us with dying *Memento's* and Time that grows old itself bids us hope no longer duration: Diuturnity is a dream and folly of expectation.

Or Sir Walter Raleigh:

> O eloquent, just, and mighty Death! whom none could advise, thou hast persuaded; what none hath dared thou hast done; and whom all the world hath flattered, thou only hast cast out of the world and despised: thou hast drawn together all the far-stretched greatness, all the pride, cruelty and ambition of man, and covered it all over with these two narrow words, *Hic jacet*.

To set these miraculous achievements of prose-music as standards for Fuller or any other writer would be unfair and absurd; but at least they may stimulate interest in his individual approach to the subject:

> Tombes [Fuller writes] are the clothes of the dead: a Grave is but a plain suit, and a rich Monument is one embroyder'd.... 'Tis a provident way to make ones Tombe in ones life-time, both hereby to prevent the negligence of heirs and to mind him of his mortality.

Fuller is by no means unmindful of human transitoriness, but his mind is also full of practical details and of illustrative anecdote:

> The shortest, plainest and truest Epitaphs are best.... Mr Cambden in his Remains presents us with examples of Great men that had little Epitaphs. And when once I ask'd a witty gentleman, an honoured friend of mine, what Epitaph was fittest to be written on Mr Cambden's Tombe. Let it be, said he,
>
> CAMDENS REMAINS.

'To want a grave,' Fuller continues, 'is the cruelty of the living, not the misery of the dead,' and then he cannot resist an anecdotal supplement:

> An English Gentleman not long since did lie on his death-bed in Spain, and the Jesuits did flock about him to pervert him to their Religion. All was in vain. Their last argument was, If you will not turn Romane Catholick, then your body shall be unburied. *Then* (answered he) *I'll stink*, and so turned his head and dyed.

But in his last paragraph Fuller contemplates his subject in a manner approaching that of his more distinguished contemporaries:

> A good Memory is the best Monument. Others are subject to Casualty and Time, and we know that the Pyramids themselves doting with age have forgotten the names of their Founders. To conclude, let us be carefull to provide rest for our souls, and our bodies will provide rest for themselves.

Fuller is not incapable of reflection upon the eternal verities, but his feet are always securely upon the ground. Rather than lose himself in an *O Altitudo*, he is the practical moralist concerned with what is here and now. *The Holy State* is, deservedly, his most popular work and, from Charles Lamb onwards, every commentator has succumbed to the temptation of stringing together examples of Fuller's oddities of exposition and illustration. Recent scholarship has also shown that *The Holy State* is more than a random assembly of aphorism and anecdote. It is planned as a treatise on the living of the good life both in the family and in the public affairs of church and state; but cheerfulness breaks in so frequently that its social philosophy tends to be obscured.

In *The Church History of Britain* Fuller is not daunted by the breadth of his canvas. He begins with 'the sad Condition of the Britons, our Predecessours, before the *Christian Faith* was preached unto them' and ends with a moving account of the death of Charles I. Through the centuries of controversy he aims at a just appraisal of conflicting views, but he never pretends to be impartial. Strongly influenced by John Fox, author of the *Book of Martyrs*, he remains a good Protestant and a good Royalist and it is from this point of view that he surveys the pageant of ecclesiastical history. When he writes of Becket, he can appreciate his strength and sanctity; but, after all, he was 'a stubborn defender of the vicious Clergy against secular Magistrates' and of his death he writes: 'A barbarous murder, and which none will go about to excuse, but much heightened both by the *Prose*, and *Poetry* (good and bad) of Popish Writers in that age.'

When he comes to the reign of Henry VIII, his sympathies are, of course, with the Reformers, but he is keenly alive to the follies of the extremists:

It happeneth in all *heights* and *heats* of oppositions, as in *horse-races*; wherein the Rider, if he doth not go beyond the *post*, cannot come to the *post*, so as to *win* the *prize*; for being upon the *speed*, he must goe beyond it that he come to it, though afterwards he may rain and turn his horse back again to the very place of the *mark*. Thus men being in the heat of contest upon the very career of their souls, because of their passions, cannot stop short at the very mark they ayme at, but some extravagancies must be indulged to humane infirmity, which in their reduced thoughts they will correct and amend.

With fanaticism and cruelty Fuller had little patience, but he was always willing to acknowledge some personal quality in his Papistical enemies. Thus, after accusing Stephen Gardiner of having a head if not a hand in the death of every eminent Protestant in Mary's reign, he acknowledges that his own great-grandmother was indebted to Gardiner for much kindness; and of Queen Mary herself he writes:

Take Queen Mary in her self abstracted from her opinions, and by her self, secluded from her bloody councellors, and her Memory will justly come under Commendation. Indeed she knew not the Art of *being popular* and never cared to learn it.... She hated to equivocate in her own Religion, and alway *was what she was*, without dissembling her judgement or Practise for fear or flattery...she had been a worthy Princesse, had as little Cruelty been done *under her*, as was done *by her*.

The ecclesiastical settlement of Elizabeth's reign was naturally more agreeable to Fuller. He remains a stout enemy of the Papists and of the more violent kind of Nonconformist, but he records with evident pleasure that the Queen endeavoured to 'embrace a middle and moderate way' with Jesuits as with Brownists.

The year of the Armada fills him with pious and patriotic gratitude and he assigns all to the goodness of God, as Queen Elizabeth did:

Leave we her in the *Quire* of *Pauls* church, devoutly on her knees...whilst going abroad, we shall finde some of her subjects worse employed in implacable enmity about Ecclesiastical discipline one against another. And let not the mentioning of this *deliverance* be censured as a deviation from the *Church-History of Britain*. Silence thereof being a sin, for had the designe took effect, neither *Protestant Church* in *Britain* had remained, nor *History* thereof been made at this present.

When he reaches the reign of Charles I, Fuller is of course writing contemporary history amidst grave uncertainty about the future. Deliberately he gives a full account of the King's coronation:

If it be *the last* Solemnitie performed on an English King in this kinde, Posteritie will conceive my paines well bestowed, because *on the last*. But if hereafter Divine providence shall assign England another King, though the transactions herein be not wholly precedentiall, something of State may be chosen out gratefull for imitation.

Throughout his long narrative the impress of Fuller's individual quality as a historian is clear. He is not afraid of short digressions and some of his most memorable characterisations occur in parentheses. Heralds, for instance, are described as 'Chemists in pedigrees to extract anything from anything'; of Sternhold and Hopkins, the versifiers of the Psalms, he notes that their piety was better than their poetry—'they had drank more of *Jordan*, than of *Helicon*'; about Matthew Parker he cannot resist a pun—'He was a *Parker* indeed, carefull to keep the fences, and shut the gates of *Discipline* against all such *Night Stealers* as would invade the same'.

'Since history', writes Professor Trevelyan, 'is our interpretation of human affairs in the past, it could not exist without bias.' Certainly Fuller had his bias, which he did not pretend to conceal. But in an age of strife and fanaticism he preserved a balance of judgment and a measure of charity that were rare amongst the controversialists of his time.

In the compilation of his last great work, *The History of the Worthies of England*, Fuller was not troubled by controversy. His design is clearly stated at the beginning:

> England may not unfitly be compared to an House not *very great*, but *convenient* and the several Shires may properly be resembled to the *rooms* thereof. Now, as learned Master *Camden* and painful Master *Speed* with others, have described the *rooms* themselves; so is it our intention, God willing, to describe the Furniture of those *rooms*; such Eminent Commodities, which every Country doth produce, with the Persons of Quality bred therein, and some other observables coincident with the same subject.

This general plan is elaborated at great length in the early chapters of the book. When he comes to speak of famous writers, it is noteworthy that Fuller proposes to include Romish exiles amongst them and that he anticipates the obvious objection:

> Grant them never so bad...their mixture cannot be infectious to others. Secondly, abate their errours, and otherwise many of them were well meriting of the Commonwealth of learning. Lastly, the passages of their lives conduce very much to the clearing of Ecclesiastical History.

Each county is treated according to the general plan —Natural Commodities—Manufactures—Buildings— Proverbs—Famous Men—Lists of Gentry and Sheriffs, and the whole narrative is enriched by Fuller's remarkable powers of memory and observation, as well as by his love of anecdote and epigram. Of Cambridgeshire he writes:

> The North-part of this *County* is lately much improved by drayning, though the poorest sort of people will not be sensible

thereof. Tell them of the great benefit to the publick, because where a Pike or Duck fed formerly, now a *Bullock* or *Sheep* is fatted, they will be ready to return, that if they be *taken* in *taking* that *Bullock* or *Sheep*, the rich Owner indicteth them for *Felons*; whereas that *Pike* or *Duck* were their own goods only for the pains of catching of them.

Of the University he does not say much, having written of it elsewhere, but he quotes a proverb: 'A boisten horse and a Cambridge Master of Arts are a couple of Creatures that will give way to nobody,' and he remarks in passing that Oxford is a University in a Town and Cambridge a Town in a University. Of course he is not always accurate. He claims Caxton (who states himself that he was born in the Weald of Kent) as a Cambridgeshire man, with no authority other than the coincidence of his name with that of a Cambridgeshire village. His last comment is on the climate:

Hard it is for *Weather* to please the *Concernments* of this *County* whose Northern part being Moist and Fenny, desires *Fair Weather*; *South* and *South-Eastern Dry* and *Heathy*, delighteth so much rain, that it can well digest (save in harvest time) one shower every *Day*, and *two* every *Sunday*. But the *God of Heaven, who can make it rain on one place and not on another*, can fit the Necessity of Both, and I remitte them both to his Providence.

Lancashire, Fuller notes, was sufficiently thick of people but exceedingly thin of Parishes.

But [he continues] for Numerosity of Chapels, surely the Church of *Manchester* exceedeth all the rest which (though anciently called but *Villa de Manchester*) is for Wealth and Greatnesse corrival with some Cities in England, having no lesse than *Nine* Chapels.

Other features noted are the Oxen ('the fairest in England') with the tips of their horns five feet apart; the manufacture of fustians, with Bolton as the staple-place, and 'as for Manchester, the *Cottons* thereof carry away the credit in our Nation, and so they did an *hundred and fifty* years agoe'; lastly, Fuller notes the fair complexions of the women, with a warning that Art may save her *pains* (not to say her *sinnes*) in endeavouring to better them.

Again, the biographical section is not wholly reliable, but at least the famous anecdote of Lawrence Chaderton deserves to be recalled. Chaderton had been 'much nuzzled in Popish Superstition', but became a famous Puritan preacher and the first Master of Emmanuel College in Cambridge. Once, on a visit to his native county, he declared at the end of a sermon of two hours' duration that he would no longer trespass upon his hearers' patience. 'Where upon,' says Fuller, 'all the Auditory cryed out "For God's sake, sir, go on, go on".'

On the first page of the *Worthies*, Fuller propounds five ends to himself: first to gain some Glory to God; secondly to preserve the memories of the Dead; thirdly, to present examples to the Living; fourthly, to entertain the Reader with Delight; and, lastly, to procure some honest profit to himself.

Here is neither false pride, nor false delicacy; with an admirable candour Fuller summarises the qualities of his own writing and these qualities were manifest in all his works. His facility for epigram and anecdote naturally secured for him popularity both as a preacher and as a commentator on the state of the nation. What is more remarkable is that he was able to preserve his individual manner of approach in his more ambitious works. No one, today, would credit Fuller with a profundity of historical or theological scholarship. But it cannot be too often insisted that *The Holy State*, the *Church History* and the *Worthies* are much more than the jottings of an antiquary with a taste for good stories. They are the product of wide reading, of industrious inquiry and of literary craftsmanship—the craftsmanship of what Fuller described as 'the general artist'. 'He was the first Englishman,' as Jessopp says, 'who with a critical instinct and a power of accumulating information, had also that measure of constructive genius which breathes life into the dry bones.'

Like Johnson, who declared that no one but a blockhead ever wrote except for money and at the same time planned *The Rambler* to promote God's glory, so Fuller was not ashamed to couple the Glory of God with profit for himself. Unlike Johnson, he wrote because he enjoyed writing, and it is this enjoyment which is communicated to his readers. More than once he comments on 'the numerosity of needless books' and then quickly recalls his own share in adding to them and the dangers of his facile pen: 'How easie is Pen and Paper piety.... I will not say it costs nothing; but it is far cheaper to work one's head than one's heart to goodness.... I can make a hundred Meditations sooner than subdue the least sin in my soul.'

In the 'troublesome and tumultuous' age in which Fuller lived controversy was paramount and no decent citizen could remain neutral. Fuller's own position was clear. Though he never concealed his enmity to ecclesiastical tyranny, whether Popish or Puritan, he pleaded always for a reasonable toleration. Similarly, in politics, he saw no reason why the liberty of the subject and the authority of parliament should not be combined with a decent reverence for the monarchy.

Today many, though not quite all, of the controversies which in Fuller's time sundered men into bitter factions have lost their relevance. As we look back over 300 years, Fuller's view frequently seems so sane, so moderate, so sensible that we wonder why more of his contemporaries could not be found to follow the *via media*. But that is because we are looking through the wrong end of the telescope. What, in 2250, will be the verdict of historians upon the fundamental differences between the advocates of Free Enterprise and the champions of the Welfare State?

Fuller lived in a revolutionary age and, as he himself sadly recognised: 'The moderate man eminent for no excess or extravagancy in his judgment will have few patrons to protect or persons to adhere unto him.'

Yet he has his reward. Oblivion may indeed have scattered her poppy over the machinations of the Jesuits and the railings of the Anabaptists; but that uniqueness which Coleridge noted in the writings of Thomas Fuller may well secure their diuturnity in the annals of literature.

II. PEPYS AND BOSWELL

SAMUEL PEPYS and JAMES BOSWELL have frequently provoked comparison. Each was the author of a classic, and the *Life of Samuel Johnson* and the *Diary* have long been admitted to the category of books which no gentleman's library should be without; they also have the much rarer distinction of being two of the most widely read and the best loved narratives in the English language.

The backgrounds of the authors and the circumstances of composition were, of course, widely different. Pepys was the son of a London tailor, though he belonged to a good Cambridgeshire family. After schooling at Huntingdon, St Paul's, and Magdalene College, Cambridge, he returned to London, married at the age of twenty-two and entered the service of his cousin, Sir Edward Montagu. That was in 1655. Five years later he began his diary. 'What rare freak of thought or circumstance', writes Sir Arthur Bryant, 'prompted him at such a moment to start to keep a diary no man will ever know.' Nor, presumably, shall we ever know with certainty whether Pepys intended the diary to be for ever shrouded in the secrecy of its shorthand. Under the terms of his will it went, as part of his library, to his old college after the death of his nephew, John Jackson, in 1723 and there it lay undisturbed for 100 years. Then, thanks to the labours of John Smith, it was deciphered and the first printed edition, containing barely half of the manuscript, appeared in 1825. The diary covered nine and a half years and was abandoned because of failing eyesight. It has rightly been hailed as a work of art, but it was a work of unpremeditated, rather than of conscious, artistry.

As he faithfully recorded, day by day, his doings and his misdoings, Pepys had no feeling that he was laying the foundations of a posthumous literary fame. Not that he was without ambition—he was very properly ambitious to be an efficient public servant, to acquire the means to establish a gentleman's household, and to make a good collection of books. In due time all these aims were achieved; but such has been the fame of the *Diary* that it is only in the present century that Pepys's great services to the state, and to the Admiralty in particular, have been fully recognised.

At once this suggests a Boswellian parallel and a Boswellian contrast. Writing in 1874 Lord Houghton remarked that 'it was the object of Boswell's life to connect his own name with that of Dr Johnson'. This is the kind of half-truth which for many years obscured the full range of Boswell's literary and social ambitions. His *Life of Samuel Johnson* was quickly recognised as the greatest biography in the language and has maintained its supremacy; but it is only in the last thirty years that Boswell has been properly estimated as an author in his own right rather than as the faithful follower of the Great Lexicographer.

Born in Edinburgh in 1740, the son of a Scotch judge, James Boswell displayed from his earliest years a passion for writing and for publicity. At the age of twenty-one he wrote an *Ode to Tragedy*; it was published anonymously but was dedicated to James Boswell, Esq. In his own words he had 'no uncommon desire for the company of men distinguished for talents and literature' and he was impervious to snubbing or ridicule. To quote his own words again:

> So not a bent sixpence cares he
> Whether *with* him or *at* him you laugh.

When at the age of twenty-three he made the Grand Tour of Europe, he discarded his letter of introduction to Rousseau and substituted one of his own. 'Put your trust', he wrote, 'in a remarkable foreigner. You will never regret it.'

One notable product of Boswell's continental tour was his book on Corsica, in the preface to which he wrote:

> He who publishes a book affecting not to be an authour, and professing an indifference for literary fame, may possibly impose upon many people such an idea of his consequence as he wishes may be received. For my part, I should be proud to be known as an authour; and I have an ardent ambition for literary fame.

Such was Boswell's deliberate apprenticeship to the profession of letters; his *Life* of Johnson was literally his masterpiece. Johnson was fifty-three years of age when Boswell was first introduced to him and for the story of those years he was involved in much 'labour and anxious attention'. For the last twenty years he relied largely upon his own diary and it is in this context that he may most fittingly be compared with Samuel Pepys.

Nothing is more characteristic of Pepys than his love of orderliness and method. He had spent 'infinite pains and time and cost...in collecting and methodising' his books and in his will enjoined that 'all possible provision should be made for [his library's] unalterable preservation and perpetual security'.

James Boswell also left instructions about his collection

of books and papers; they were not in such good order, but they were of vast proportions, for Boswell seldom destroyed anything. He not only preserved the letters he received, but frequently made copies of those he wrote; he kept intermittent diaries and stored an immense collection of memoranda, of newspapers containing contributions of his own, and of documents of every kind. And it was all deliberate; however intimate, it was all to be available some day for publication. But the day was long in coming. The whole collection was bequeathed to Sir William Forbes, the Reverend W. J. Temple and Edmond Malone, with 'discretionary power to publish more or less'. Forbes and Malone examined the papers and decided to do nothing for the time being. In 1822, when James Boswell the younger died, a few scraps of his father's manuscripts were sold and for more than 100 years it was firmly believed that the great mass of Boswell's papers had been destroyed. The belief was strengthened by the failure of Birkbeck Hill and other Johnsonian scholars to obtain any information from the Boswell family.

The story of the successive discoveries of the Boswell papers is one of the most romantic and astonishing episodes of literary history. The first act in the drama was a mere accident: a Major Stone making a purchase in a small shop in Boulogne in 1850 noted that his purchase was being wrapped in a letter written in English and that the signature at the end of the letter was that of James Boswell. The stock of wrapping-papers was traced and Major Stone bought the lot. The bundle contained about 100 letters written by Boswell to his friend W. J. Temple, one of his three executors.

But it was not until seventy years later that the real harvest began. In the 1920's rumours began to circulate that the Boswell MSS. had not, after all, been destroyed, but that they were reposing at Malahide Castle, County Dublin, the home of the late Lord Talbot de Malahide, a great-great-grandson on his mother's side, of James Boswell.

At this point I interject a brief personal reminiscence. In June 1926, I had the good fortune to visit Lord Talbot, who laid out for my inspection just a few samples of the manuscripts in his possession—there was Goldsmith's reply to Boswell's letter of congratulation on the production of *She Stoops to Conquer*, there was Boswell's account of his interview with George III and other fascinating items. Later in the same month another visitor arrived at Malahide—the late Colonel Ralph Isham, an enthusiast, who was interested not only in investigation but in purchase. By the end of 1927 he had acquired the whole series of Boswell papers (now known as 'the first Malahide find') and these were published in a limited edition between 1928 and 1934.

For the third act in the drama of discovery the scene was shifted. In 1930 Professor C. C. Abbott, searching for material relating to James Beattie among Sir William Forbes' papers at Fettercairn House, Kincardineshire, came upon a collection of Boswellian documents amounting to about 1600 items, among them Boswell's famous *London Journal* of 1762–3. Legal difficulties arose about the release of these documents, but they were eventually secured by Colonel Isham together with a second Malahide find containing material of the greatest importance. The whole collection, with the addition of other manuscripts subsequently discovered, was purchased by Yale University in 1949 and is now being given to the world in annual instalments.

Even the briefest account of the extraordinary series of Boswellian discoveries may serve to emphasise the difference between Pepys's diary and the Boswell journals from a purely quantitative point of view. Pepys's diary is a neat and orderly document embodying the detail of nine and a half years; Boswell's journals, letters and memoranda sprawl over forty years. No longer is it true to say, as Tanner said, that 'we have more intimate knowledge of Pepys than of any other personality of the past'. Pepys's diary has been described as an indiscretion of his youth; Boswell's papers reveal the improprieties of a lifetime.

This is, indeed, the outstanding difference between the careers of the two men: the record of Pepys's later life is the record of supremely successful and valuable service in Parliament and in naval administration; Boswell, too, aimed at distinction at the bar and longed to enter the House of Commons, but in this he failed miserably; it was only in his literary ambitions that he achieved fulfilment —an achievement which is the more remarkable as the full story of Boswell's way of life is revealed. For to the end he persistently failed to resist the allurements of wine and women, and it is sometimes difficult to imagine how his hours of sobriety sufficed for the compilation of his biographical masterpiece. Pepys, too, in his younger days frequently drank too much—but not on the Boswellian scale.

Home and to bed [he recorded on 9 March 1660]. All night troubled in my thoughts how to order my business upon this great change with me that I could not sleep and being over-heated with drink I made a promise the next morning to drink no strong drink this week, for I find that it makes me sweat and puts me quite out of order.

Again on 29 September 1661:

I drink I know not how, of my own accord, so much wine that I was even almost foxed and my head aked all night; so home and to bed, without prayers, which I never did yet, since I came to the house, of a Sunday night: I being now so out of order that I durst not read prayers for fear of being perceived by my servants in what case I was. So to bed.

So, on the last day of the year, he took a solemn oath to abstain from plays and wine and found himself much better for it, but in February he had reason to fear that 'by my too sudden leaving off wine, I do contract many evils upon myself'.

With the stories of Pepys's infidelities all readers of the *Diary* are familiar. Mrs Pepys was not unnaturally suspicious of Mrs Martin, Mrs Pierce, Mrs Knipp and the rest, and when she caught her husband in October 1668 in the act of embracing Deb, it occasioned the greatest sorrow to Pepys that ever he knew in this world. But three weeks later he contrived to meet Deb again in a coach and told his wife a 'fair tale' when he got home. But Mrs Pepys was not deceived, and after a stormy scene Pepys promised never to offend more, praying God for grace more and more every day to fear him and to be true to his poor wife. But, alas, Pepys's promises were tinged with a Boswellian frailty. Pepys could never resist a pretty face, but he had no feeling for promiscuity. Boswell ranged over a wider field. 'I ought to be a Turk,' he once wrote, 'I believe I should make a very good Sultan', and in the *Journals* already published which record his early adventures in London, Holland, Germany, France and Italy his innumerable affairs, whether with countesses or with drabs are described with a frankness of detail far exceeding the confessions of Pepys.

With Boswell it was no mere sowing of wild oats. He married a good woman and was conscious of her goodness; but except for comparatively short periods he never attained to a self-control sufficient to make him live a decent life. The Edinburgh journal of the 1770's is a wearisome record of drunkenness and debauchery, relieved only by Boswell's extraordinary candour. Thus on 28 August 1776 he writes:

I drank too much. We had whist after dinner. When I returned to town, I was a good deal intoxicated, ranged the streets, and having met with a κομελy, φρεσχ-λοοκινγ γιrλ, μαδλy υευτυρεδ to λγε *witχ* χερ... I told my δεαρ *W*ιφε immediately.

It is the last sentence that is so characteristically Boswellian—and so unlike Pepys. Similarly, on 10 April 1780:

Dined at Dr Gillespie's with Commissioner Cochrane, Dr Webster and John. Was in sound spirits, but drank so as to be intoxicated a good deal, so that I ranged an hour in the street and dallied with ten strumpets. I had however caution enough left not to run a risk with them. Told my valuable spouse when I came home. She was good humoured and gave me excellent beef soup, which lubricated me and made me well.

Poor Mrs Boswell! She had married with her eyes open, but she can hardly have been prepared for all that she had to endure. She read her husband's journal from time to time and in principle disapproved of it. Even Boswell had doubts sometimes. On 30 July 1779 he wrote:

Were my Journal to be discovered and made publick in my own lifetime, how shocking would it be to me! And after my death, would it not hurt my children? I must not be so plain. I will write to Dr Johnson on the subject.

But whatever Dr Johnson said, Boswell adhered to his policy of self-revelation. 'I have a kind of strange feeling', he wrote, 'as if I wished nothing to be secret that concerns myself.'

Boswell's persistent intemperance in relation both to wine and women must not blind us to the brilliance of his reporting. The diaries that he kept during his visits to London are, in fact, the core of his immortal biography and his description of evenings at the Club, or at the Mitre, or at a dinner-party of which Johnson was the central figure are, by general consent, the high-lights of the work.

Johnson apart, there are many passages in Boswell's earlier journals in which the ingenuousness and the careful observation of detail may well be reminiscent of Pepys.

In 1769 Boswell, fresh from his tour abroad and full of enthusiasm for the cause of Corsican liberty, decided to attend the Shakespeare Festival at Stratford-on-Avon, taking with him the costume of a Corsican chief to wear at the masked ball.

6 Sept. 1769: To see a noble band of the first musicians from London, with Dr Arne at their head, Mr Garrick, a number of nobility and gentry and of the learned and ingenious assembled to do honour to Shakespeare in his native place gave me much satisfaction....

At dinner...an Irish lady, wife of Captain Sheldon, a most agreeable little woman, pleased me most. I got into great spirits. I paid her particular attention. I began to imagine that she was stealing me from my valuable spouse. I was most unhappy from this imagination. I rose and went near the Orchestra, and looked stedfastly at that beautiful insinuating creature, Mrs Baddeley of Drury Lane, and in an instant Mrs Sheldon was effaced. I then saw that what I feared was love was in reality nothing more than transient liking. It had no intereference with my noble attachment....

7 Sept: This was the night of the Ball in Mask, when I was to appear as a Corsican chief. I had begun some verses for the Jubilee in that character. But I could not finish them. I was quite impatient. I went home and forced myself to exertion and at last finished what I intended. I then ran to Garrick, read them to him and found him much pleased. He said the passage as to himself—

'Had Garrick, who Dame Nature's pencil stole
Just where old Shakespeare dropt it, etc—'

was both a fine poetical image and a fine compliment. There was a fellow called Fulke Weale here, who advertised printing at an hour's notice, I suppose taking it for granted that Stratford would produce a general poetical inspiration which would exert itself every hour. To him I went. But Mr Angelo's fireworks turned his head, and made him idle. He preferred them to all poetical fire. I then went to the Bookseller and Printer of the Place, Mr Kaiting. He had a lad from Baskerville's at Birmingham, of Scots extraction, his name *Shank*. I found him a clever active fellow; and set him to work directly. He brought me a proof to the Masquerade Ball about two in the morning. But could not get my verses thrown off in time for me to give them about in my Corsican dress. I was quite happy at the Masquerade. I had been at a Publick Breakfast in the Town Hall, and had tea made for me by my pretty Irish lady, who no longer disturbed me. Tonight she did me the favour to dance with me a minuet while I was in complete armour, and, when I laid aside my arms, a country dance. I got acquainted with Mr Murphy, Mr Colman, Mr Kelly, Mr Foote at this Jubilee...My Corsican dress attracted everybody. I was as much a favourite as I could desire.

It would be difficult to select a happier portrait of the young Boswell than this. At about the same age, on 10 April 1661, Pepys went on an expedition with Sir Wm Batten and others to see the Dockhouses at Chatham. After being hospitably received by Mr Pett and having inspected the good ship *The Prince*, the party went on to Rochester

and there saw the Cathedrall which is now fitting for use and the organ then a-tuning, Then away thence, observing the great doors of the church which, they say, was covered with the skins of the Danes.... So to the Salutacion tavern, where Mr Alcock and many of the town came and entertained us with wine and oysters and other things.... Here much mirth... we had, for my sake, two fiddles, the one a base viall, on which he that played, played well some lyra lessons, but both together made the worst musique that ever I heard.

We had a fine collacion, but I took little pleasure in that, for the illness of the musique and for the intentness of my mind upon Mrs Rebecca Allen. After we had done eating, the ladies went to dance and among the men we had, I was forced to dance too; and did make an ugly shift. Mrs R. Allen danced very well and seems the best humoured woman that ever I saw. About 9 o'clock Sir William and my lady went home, and we continued dancing an hour or two, and so broke up very pleasant and merry, and so walked home, I leading Mrs Rebecca, who seemed, I know not why, in that and other things, to be desirous of my favours and would in all things show me respects. Going home, she would needs have me sing, and I did pretty well and was highly esteemed by them. So to Captain Allen's... and there, having no mind to leave Mrs Rebecca what with talk and singing.... Mrs Turner and I staid there till 2 o'clock in the morning and was most exceeding merry and I had the opportunity of kissing Mrs Rebecca very often....

There is a notable kinship of spirit between these two passages. There is the same pleasure in being a member of a congenial company that is out to enjoy itself; there is the same zest for sightseeing; there is the same appreciation of the pleasures of the table; there is the same enjoyment of flirtation; and there is the same satisfaction in being a popular member of the party. But there is one difference: Pepys, of course, is delighted that Mrs Rebecca should show him such marked favour; but he is quite honest in saying that he did not understand why he should be singled out for such attentions. Boswell, on the other hand, deliberately set out to attract attention. As always, he was dramatising himself. His enthusiasm for Corsican liberty was genuine enough, but he chose to advertise it in a flagrantly ridiculous way. Ridicule he did not mind, provided that he achieved sufficient prominence and that he enlarged his acquaintance with well-known people. 'I was as much a favourite as I could desire'—such was his verdict on the Stratford-on-Avon expedition; for Boswell it was the final, and completely satisfying, verdict and something quite different from Pepys's naïve acceptance of unpremeditated enjoyment.

Not that Pepys was averse from recording his own successes. In his orderly manner he frequently contemplates his steady rise in the world and his record, for instance, of his famous speech in the House of Commons of March 1667/8 bears no mark of false modesty. Having fortified himself with half a pint of mulled sack and a dram of brandy he spoke most acceptably and smoothly for more than three hours, during which many went out to dinner and came back half drunk. But there was a chorus of praise for the speech; the Solicitor-General said that

Pepys 'spoke the best of any man in England; the King himself congratulated him; Mr George Montagu said he was another Cicero...'. If Boswell had ever approached such success in his career as an advocate, we can well imagine that he would have preserved a similar record of complimentary remarks. But he would not have added, as Pepys did, 'for which the Lord God make me thankful! and that I may make use of it not to pride and vain-glory, but that, now I have this esteem, I may do nothing that may lessen it'.

It was only as an author that Boswell tasted the sweets of universal praise: 'My book has amazing celebrity,' he wrote to Temple after the publication of his book on Corsica in 1768, 'Lord Lyttelton, Mr Walpole, Mrs Macaulay, Mr Garrick have all written me noble letters about it'; and when the *Life* of Johnson had been published in May 1791 he wrote in the following month to John Wilkes: 'You said to me yesterday of my *magnum opus* "it is a wonderful book". Do confirm this to me, so as I may have your *testimonium* in my archives at Auchinleck.'

Pepys, from the very beginning of his public career, was an industrious apprentice and in due time he had his reward. One of his outstanding virtues as a civil servant was his extremely methodical ordering of business; this love of method was similarly evident in the ordering of his household as poor Mrs Pepys found to her cost; and when Pepys gradually secured the leisure and the means to gratify his passion as a collector of books and manuscripts and prints and music, he proceeded in the same orderly manner: 'Up & by & by to my bookseller's, and there did give thorough direction for the new binding of a great many of my old books, to make my whole study of the same binding, within very few' he wrote on 18 January 1665 and three weeks later he noted what a pleasant sight it was to contemplate the uniform appearance of his shelves. But he was not a collector of the omnivorous type. On 2 February 1667 he spent a Sunday morning in setting his books in order and like all collectors he discovered a considerable increase in the course of the year. But he was determined to discipline his library: 'I am fain', he wrote, 'to lay by several books to make room for better, being resolved to keep no more than just my presses will contain.' He was as methodical in destruction as in preservation. At Christmas time 1664 he judged it fit to look over all his books and papers and to tear up all that he found either boyish or not to be worth keeping or fit to be seen, if it should please God to take him away suddenly. Nearly a year before he had made a similar clearance, destroying, in particular, the MS. of *Love a Cheate*, a romance which he had begun ten years before at Cambridge. 'Reading it over,' he writes, 'I liked it very well and wondered a little at myself at my vein at that time when I wrote it, doubting that I cannot do so well now if I would try.'

All this is very unlike Boswell. It is true that occasionally Boswell contemplated some specific field of collecting. Thus on 13 September 1776 he wrote about his trip to Glasgow: 'I went to the College and bought a few little books at Foulis' shop and amused myself with a project of purchasing a compleat collection of the productions of the press of the ingenious brothers, both now dead.' But this was just a passing fancy. What Boswell collected was *Boswelliana*.

The primary point of resemblance between Pepys and Boswell lies in the fact that neither hesitated to enter in his diary the least creditable features of his life and character, though for the most lurid passages each was driven to a prudent measure of disguise—Pepys to an Anglo-French jargon, Boswell to a Greek transliteration. Each of them was religious in his own way; each of them fell short of the moral standards which his religion enjoined; each of them, when attending divine service, was liable to concentrate his attention upon pretty women. From the social point of view, it is clear that each of them possessed the indefinable and unteachable quality which is commonly called charm. Through his *Diary* Pepys has communicated this charm to generations of readers and there is little need, at this time, to analyse it. Boswell's case is less simple. For many years the paradox of the greatest biography being written by a man of Boswell's character served to baffle the critics. Macaulay's preposterous theory that Boswell wrote a great book because he was a great fool dominated the popular view for many years, but is now very properly discredited. The *Life* of Johnson is, in fact, the product not only of descriptive brilliance, but of patient and industrious research. Despite his drunkenness, despite his frequently nauseating accounts of his sexual licence, there is abundant evidence of Boswell's essentially clubable qualities, of the good humour which made him irresistible in a social milieu. In her famous mark-book[1] Mrs Thrale gave Johnson full marks (20) for Morality and 0 for Good Humour; to Boswell she gave, rather charitably, 5 for Morality, but 19 for Good Humour. As

[1] See p. 68.

a final fragment of evidence on this point a paragraph from an unpublished letter of Boswell may be cited. It is a letter written to his cousin Robert Boswell from Eton on 30 July 1792, at the end of his son Alexander's last term at school:

> I am here at the delivery of my son Alexander from school. He hastens off to London to-day. But I hover here awhile to contemplate a noble Seminary, which I regret much my not having had the advantage to attend. The Provost and Fellows are wonderfully good to me. This is what is called Election time when the boys are chosen for the foundation at King's College, Cambridge; and there is a deal of feasting in which I share; for they are pleased to hold me as an Etonian by adoption. I own I like the union of luxury and learning.

Boswell was nearing the end of his dissolute life, but it is clear that the Provost and Fellows of Eton were captivated. The charm—a charm of Pepysian quality—was still at work.

III. DOCTOR JOHNSON

1. *THE MORALIST*[1]

HOLY WEEK 1778. On Monday Johnson dined at Bennet Langton's, in company with Boswell, Dr Porteus (Bishop of Chester), and Dr Stinton (Chaplain to the Archbishop of Canterbury). Before dinner Johnson was silent. Later he talked of Horatian syntax and of literary style. Topham Beauclerk came in afterwards and Johnson and Boswell stayed to supper. Reference was made to a wish once expressed by Dr Dodd to be a member of the Club. 'I should be sorry', said Johnson, 'if any of our club were hanged. I will not say but some of them deserve it.'

On Tuesday Johnson dined at General Oglethorpe's, with General Paoli, Bennet Langton, and Boswell. Having, as usual, spoken in defence of luxury, Johnson was led to a discussion of forms of government: 'The more contracted that power is,' he declared, 'the more easily it is destroyed. A country governed by a despot is an inverted cone.' From political theory he passed to an examination of the etymology of macaronic verses.

On Wednesday there was rather a larger dinner-party at Mr Dilly's. The company included Mrs Knowles, the Quakeress, Miss Seward (the Swan of Lichfield), Dr Mayo (the dissenting minister whose courage in remaining unmoved by Johnson's blows earned him the name of the Literary Anvil), Mr Beresford (tutor to the Duke of Bedford), Boswell, and Johnson. Before dinner Johnson was deep in Charles Sheridan's recently published *Account*

[1] Annual Lecture on a Master Mind, British Academy, 1944.

of the late Revolution in Sweden, so deep that he took the book to the table with him and wrapped it in the tablecloth with a view to reading it between the courses. Not that the dinner was neglected—indeed, an early topic of conversation was cookery and cookery books. 'I could write a better book of cookery', Johnson boasted, 'than has ever yet been written; it should be a book upon philosophical principles.' From cookery Johnson went on to describe how he had acted as literary agent for an English Benedictine's translation of the Duke of Berwick's memoirs and then to argue with Mrs Knowles about the limits of feminine freedom. Questioned by Dr Mayo, Johnson gave his opinion of Soame Jenyns's *View of the Internal Evidence of the Christian Religion*: 'I think it a pretty book; not very theological indeed.' From this followed a discussion of friendship as a Christian virtue: 'Christianity', said Johnson, 'recommends universal benevolence, to consider all men as our brethren.... Surely, Madam, your sect must approve of this; for you call all men *friends*.' 'We are commanded to do good to all men', replied Mrs Knowles, 'but especially to them who are of the household of Faith', and, when Johnson commented that the household was wide enough, 'But Doctor', said Mrs Knowles, 'our Saviour had twelve Apostles, yet there was *one* whom he *loved*. John was called "the disciple whom Jesus loved"'. At which Johnson's eyes sparkled with benignant admiration: 'Very well, indeed, Madam. You have said very well.'

But upon this pleasant atmosphere of felicitation a sudden storm broke: 'I am willing to love all mankind', roared Johnson in a voice which Boswell felt might be heard across the Atlantic, 'except an American.' 'Pray,

Sir', said Dr Mayo after Boswell had successfully effected a diversion, 'have you read Edwards, of New England, on Grace?' 'No, Sir', replied Johnson. One feels that Dr Mayo might more suitably have chosen a theologian nearer home. Soon, however, Johnson was drawn into a discussion of Free Will. All theory was against it, he said, all experience for it. Again he defended luxury, criticising Mandeville for reckoning among the vices everything that gives pleasure. Pleasure was not necessarily a vice, though many individual pleasures were vicious. The happiness of heaven would be that pleasure and virtue would be perfectly consistent. Meanwhile the happiness of society must depend upon virtue. A disparaging reference having been made to William Mason, Johnson was ready with an explanation: 'Mason's a Whig.' 'What! a Prig, Sir?' said Mrs Knowles, not hearing distinctly. 'Worse, Madam; a Whig! But he is both.'

More serious talk was to follow. When Boswell expressed horror at the thought of death, Mrs Knowles replied that it was the gate of life. Johnson was not to be so easily comforted. Standing upon the hearth and gloomily rolling about, he declared: 'No rational man can die without uneasy apprehension.' A long argument followed, with Johnson concluding: 'The lady confounds annihilation, which is nothing, with the apprehension of it, which is dreadful.' The talk turned to John Wesley and his ghost story, and Johnson set great importance upon ghost stories. Finally, he was roused to quite disproportionate indignation concerning a young lady's conversion to Quakerism. The ladies of the company were shocked by his vehemence.

'We remained together', writes Boswell, 'till it was pretty late. Notwithstanding occasional explosions of violence, we were all delighted upon the whole with Johnson.'

Here is the familiar Johnson as portrayed in some of the most brilliant pages of Boswell's social chronicle, pages which present a microcosm of Johnson's opinions and prejudices and show him discussing cookery books and the eternal verities with equal gusto. It is Johnson as we most frequently and most naturally think of him. If we accept Sir Max Beerbohm's division of mankind into the two classes of hosts and guests, there can be no doubt of the category into which Johnson will fall. He was one of the great guests of history—not that he could be relied upon to be charming, or even civil. But to have Johnson as a guest was to bring distinction upon the party. There might, of course, be an element of speculation. Would he talk and would he talk well? Anger and contradictory violence were not feared; the fear was that he might not talk at all. It was a fear that was not often realised.

But dictatorship of the dinner-table did not constitute the whole Johnson. On the Good Friday following the series of dinner-parties Johnson, accompanied by Boswell, followed his usual practice of attending divine service at St Clement Danes. They had, as usual, talked too long after breakfast and arrived at church late—at the second lesson in fact. But on the return from this service there occurred an encounter that was unusual. It was with Oliver Edwards, who had been an undergraduate with Johnson at Pembroke College, Oxford. It was when they had reached Johnson's house that Mr Edwards delivered himself of his immortal apologia: 'You are a philosopher, Dr Johnson. I have tried too in my time to be a philosopher; but, I don't know how, cheerfulness was always breaking in.' Mr Edwards's personal confession has established itself so firmly in the affections of generations of readers that his opening words are apt to be forgotten. 'You are a philosopher, Dr Johnson'—not 'You are a famous man of letters', not 'You are the Great Lexicographer'; but 'You are a philosopher'. It was forty-nine years since the two men had met. Edwards had practised successfully as a Chancery lawyer and had retired to a farm in the country. From time to time he had read about Johnson in the newspapers; from time to time, no doubt, he had dipped into the pages of *Rasselas* or *The Rambler*. He was, literally, the man in the street and instinctively he addressed Johnson as a philosopher. It is a reputation which Johnson has not maintained. Historians of English thought pay but scant attention to him, and the late Professor Alexander concluded that he was very little of a philosopher in the stricter sense of the term. Certainly no one would argue that Johnson was a metaphysician. Philosophy, according to Berkeley, was nothing else but the study of wisdom and truth, and of philosophy in this sense Johnson might well claim to be an assiduous student; but when he was confronted with Berkeley's theory of the non-existence of Matter, he disposed of it in the manner of the Grand Philistine. It is indeed to be feared that Johnson never applied his mind to an examination of what Berkeley's theory implied; for Berkeley did not deny the existence of a stone which could be kicked; what he denied was the existence of Matter which could neither be kicked nor apprehended by any other human sense. But Johnson was not primarily interested in definitions of reality. The miseries of human life had for him a reality which made him impatient of a discussion whether a chair which he had just seen in a room had an existence of its own after he had left the room and shut the door. Philosophy interested Johnson only in its application to human conduct and human happiness; and when Soame Jenyns endeavoured to justify the dictum 'whatever is, is right' by maintaining that the sufferings of individuals were necessary to universal happiness, Johnson had little difficulty in demolishing an argument which ended, as he said, 'in belief that for the Evils of life there is some good reason and in confession that the reason cannot be found'.

What Mr Edwards meant, in short, was that Johnson was a moralist. Fifty years before their chance encounter, Johnson had arrived at Oxford as a freshman of exceptionally wide reading and scholastic promise. His scheme of study was grandiose; also, after a reading of Law's *Serious Call*, he began to think in earnest about religion. At the end of four terms he had come down—the scholar *manqué*. Poverty, ill health, and the idleness of melancholia militated against the achievement of scholastic ambition. Two courses were open to him—school-mastering and journalism—and he tried them both. When he arrived in London with $2\frac{1}{2}d.$ in his pocket in 1737, he entered into the life of Grub Street without a whine. Three years earlier he had issued Proposals for an edition of the Latin works of Politian, together with a history of modern Latin poetry from Petrarch to Politian; he had also written to Edward Cave, founder and editor of *The Gentleman's Magazine*, offering him 'short literary dissertations in Latin or English, critical remarks on authors ancient or modern...' and suggesting that such pieces might be preferable to 'low jests, aukward buffoonery, or the dull scurrilities of either party'. From the beginning, Johnson's approach to literature is that of the moralist as well as of the scholar. Cave, of whom it is recorded that 'he had no great relish for mirth, but could bear it', was Johnson's employer, in the gallery of the House of Commons and elsewhere, for many years. It was he who printed, for publication by Robert Dodsley, Johnson's first poem, *London*, a poem which is a passionate attack upon corruption at home and appeasement abroad. Juvenal was the master-moralist whom he delighted to follow in painting his picture of the metropolis:

> Here Malice, Rapine, Accident conspire,
> And now a Rabble rages, now a Fire;
> Their Ambush here relentless Ruffians lay,
> And here the fell Attorney prowls for Prey;
> Here falling Houses thunder on your Head,
> And here a female Atheist talks you dead...
> On Thames's Banks, in silent Thought we stood,
> Where Greenwich smiles upon the silver Flood:
> Struck with the Seat that gave Eliza Birth,
> We Kneel, and kiss the consecrated Earth;
> In pleasing Dreams the blissful Age renew,
> And call Britannia's Glories back to view;
> Behold her Cross triumphant on the Main,
> The Guard of Commerce, and the Dread of Spain
> Ere Masquerades debauch'd, Excise oppress'd,
> Or English Honour grew a standing Jest.

It was the same moralist that wrote *The Vanity of Human Wishes* more than ten years later, but it was a moralist with a greater breadth of vision and a greater maturity of style. *London* is dated; it is unmistakably a poem of the year 1738. *The Vanity of Human Wishes,* on the other hand, still makes its appeal, untrammelled by the time or place of its composition:

> On what foundation stands the warrior's pride,
> How just his hopes let Swedish Charles decide;
> A frame of adamant, a soul of fire,
> No dangers fright him, and no labours tire;
> O'er love, o'er fear, extends his wide domain,
> Unconquer'd lord of pleasure and of pain;
> No joys to him pacific scepters yield,
> War sounds the trump, he rushes to the field;
> Behold surrounding kings their pow'r combine,
> And one capitulate, and one resign;
> Peace courts his hand, but spreads her charms in vain;
> 'Think nothing gain'd, he cries, till nought remain,
> 'On Moscow's walls till Gothic standards fly,
> 'And all be mine beneath the polar sky.'
> The march begins in military state,
> And nations on his eye suspended wait;
> Stern Famine guards the solitary coast,
> And Winter barricades the realms of Frost;
> He comes, not want and cold his course delay;—
> Hide, blushing Glory, hide Pultowa's day;
> The vanquish'd hero leaves his broken bands,
> And shews his miseries in distant lands;
> Condemn'd a needy supplicant to wait,
> While ladies interpose, and slaves debate.
> But did not Chance at length her error mend?
> Did no subverted empire mark his end?
> Did rival monarchs give the fatal wound?
> Or hostile millions press him to the ground?
> His fall was destin'd to a barren strand,
> A petty fortress, and a dubious hand;
> He left the name, at which the world grew pale,
> To point a moral, or adorn a tale.

The history of Charles XII was modern history in Johnson's day, but Johnson has lifted it into the category of the universal.

That the moralist is fully displayed in the author of *The Rambler* needs no emphasis. More than any work, except possibly *Rasselas*, *The Rambler* embodied in Boswell's mind the spirit of the essential Johnson. When he set out on his grand tour, he told Johnson that *The Rambler* should accompany him round Europe; when the lively pretty little woman sat on Johnson's knee at Corrichatachin, it was 'highly comick' in Boswell's eyes that 'the grave philosopher—the Rambler' should toy with a Highland beauty; when Johnson displayed a somewhat excessive enjoyment of his own joke over the making of Bennet Langton's will, Boswell found the pleasantry 'certainly not such as might be expected from the author of *The Rambler*'.

Johnson composed a special prayer when he embarked upon *The Rambler*, and for Boswell, as for Mr Edwards and many other contemporaries, Johnson was primarily the majestic exponent of ethical wisdom. The first academic recognition which he received was the degree of Master of Arts from the University of Oxford. The occasion was the imminent publication of the Dictionary; but the Chancellor, in proposing the degree to Convocation, dwelt first upon Johnson as 'having very eminently distinguished himself by the publication of a series of essays, excellently calculated to form the manners of the people, and in which the cause of religion and morality is everywhere maintained by the strongest powers of argument and language'.

But while the moralist flourished, the scholar was not

idle. The first announcement of the edition of Shakespeare was issued in 1745 and the *Plan* of the Dictionary two years later. Always, in this early part of his career, Johnson was conscious first of his lack of academical qualifications, secondly of his capacity for scholarly criticism and research, and thirdly of the necessity of being a professional author—in no other way could he earn his living. He did not complain. From time to time, it is true, he would write with a certain grimness of the hopes and fears, the ambitions and disappointments of the author's life:

Thus in the 145th number of *The Rambler* he writes:

It is the proper ambition of the heroes in literature to enlarge the boundaries of knowledge by discovering and conquering new regions of the intellectual world. To the success of such undertakings perhaps some degree of fortuitous happiness is necessary which no man can promise or procure to himself; and therefore doubt and irresolution may be forgiven in him that ventures into the unexplored abysses of truth and attempts to find his way through the fluctuations of uncertainty and the conflicts of contradiction.

Again Johnson, who was bred among books, who tore the heart out of a book with unflagging voracity, who was born, as someone said, to grapple with great libraries, could contemplate the collective monuments of book-production with the dispassionate realism of the detached observer:

No place [he wrote in the 106th *Rambler*] affords a more striking conviction of the vanity of human hopes, than a publick library; for who can see the wall crowded on every side by mighty volumes, the works of laborious meditation, and accurate enquiry, now scarcely known but by the catalogue and preserved only to increase the pomp of learning, without considering how many hours have been wasted in vain endeavours, how often imagination has anticipated the praises of futurity.... Of the innumerable authors whose performances are thus treasured up in magnificent obscurity most are forgotten because they never deserved to be remembered.

Johnson himself was engaged upon a work of truly heroic proportions. It is nearly 200 years since the proposal for a Dictionary was brought before Johnson by a syndicate of book-sellers, and the science of lexicography has undergone such changes in that period that what remains of the Dictionary in most memories is purely anecdotal. Everyone remembers the definitions of Oats, of Excise, of Lexicographer, of Network, while the Dictionary itself tends to be 'treasured up in magnificent obscurity'. But if anyone is in doubt about the quality or the magnitude of Johnson's achievement, let him first of all examine what was the standard English dictionary immediately before Johnson signed his contract with the booksellers—the *Universal Etymological English Dictionary* of Nathaniel Bailey, first published in 1721; let him then turn to Johnson's *Plan*, of which the chief purpose was 'to preserve the purity and ascertain the meaning of our English idiom'. The selection of words, their spelling and pronunciation, their etymology and derivation, their variety of usage; 'the labour of interpreting these words and phrases with brevity, fulness and perspicuity'; and finally the illustration of these usages by quotations from the best writers of English prose and verse—these were the tasks which Johnson set before himself. Though his aim was to standardize the English language, he was fully conscious that he was dealing not with dead bones, but with living matter:

Words [he wrote] when they are not gaining strength...
are generally losing it. Though art may sometimes prolong
their duration, it will rarely give them perpetuity; and their
changes will be almost always informing us, that language is
the work of man, of a being from whom permanence and
stability cannot be derived.

With this ideal of flexibility clearly in his mind,
Johnson endeavoured, as he said in his *Preface*, 'to proceed with a scholar's reverence for antiquity and a grammarian's regard to the genius of our tongue'; he did not
forget that *words are the daughters of earth and that things
are the sons of heaven*. Nor did he forget that if he aimed
at too high a standard of exactitude and completeness, his
work would never be done at all:

I saw that one inquiry only gave occasion to another, that
book referred to book, that to search was not always to find, and
to find was not always to be informed....I then contracted my
design, determining to confide in myself, and no longer to
solicit auxiliaries, which produced more encumbrance than
assistance; by this I obtained at least one advantage, that I set
limits to my work, which would in time be ended, though not
completed.

'Determining to confide in myself.' There is nothing of
arrogance, nothing of complacency, in this phrase of
Johnson's. It is based, first, upon a healthy reliance
upon his own scholarship and, secondly, upon his firsthand knowledge of the requirements of editors and
publishers.

'A child is whipp'd and gets his task and there's an end
on't', he had said in another context; and he knew that the
same was true of authors of riper years. Had Johnson

been engaged—and endowed—to compile the Dictionary within the shelter of academic bowers, it would have been many more than eight years before the last sheet went to press.

Despite small blemishes [wrote Sir James Murray], the dictionary was a marvellous piece of work to accomplish in eight and a half years; and it is quite certain that if all the quotations had had to be verified and furnished with exact references, a much longer time, or the employment of much more collaboration, would have been required. With much antecedent, with much skilled co-operation, and with strenuous effort, it took more than nine years to produce the first three letters of the alphabet of the Oxford New English Dictionary.

Finally, let the inquirer turn to the Dictionary itself, or to one letter of it for a sample, say the letter G: Bailey devotes twenty-four small octavo pages to the letter, Johnson seventy-seven pages in folio. On the first page the little word GAD may catch the eye. Bailey devotes two lines to its definition—'to ramble, rove, range or straggle about'. Johnson's definition is similar, but is supplemented by quotations from *Romeo and Juliet*, Ecclesiasticus, Bacon's *Essays*, George Herbert, Milton, Dryden, L'Estrange, and Locke. This little group of writers is fairly typical. Page after page will be found to contain nine or ten passages from Shakespeare; Dryden is frequently a good second; and Locke appears on nearly every page. The contrast with Bailey is even better illustrated by the word GO. Bailey, as usual, is brief, defining the word 'to walk, move, &c.' Johnson distinguishes sixty-seven senses of the word, including a certain number of combinations, such as 'Go about', 'Go down', 'Go off' and such like. There are about thirty quotations from

Shakespeare, about the same number from the Authorized Version, fourteen from Locke, eleven from Dryden, ten from Swift, nine from Addison, eight from Bacon; and in his 68th paragraph Johnson concludes: 'The senses of this word are very indistinct; its general notion is motion or progression.' One further example may be quoted from the letter G—the definition of the not very elegant verb 'to gargle'; 'To wash the throat with some liquor not suffered immediately to descend', a little triumph, surely, of delicacy and precision.

Johnson was under no illusion about the making of dictionaries. He knew and recorded that while it was hastening to publication some words were budding and some were falling away. He had grappled with his task like a master-builder and time has not tarnished the sonorous dignity with which he offered his work to the world:

In this work, when it shall be found that much is omitted, let it not be forgotten that much likewise is performed; and that though no book was ever spared out of tenderness to the author and the world is little solicitous to know whence proceeded the faults of that which it condemns; yet it may gratify curiosity to inform it that the English Dictionary was written with little assistance of the learned, and without any patronage of the great; not in the soft obscurities of retirement, or under the shelter of academick bowers, but amidst inconvenience and distraction, in sickness and in sorrow... I have protracted my work till most of those whom I wished to please, have sunk into the grave, and success and miscarriage are empty sounds; I, therefore, dismiss it with frigid tranquillity, having little to fear or hope from censure or from praise.

When the last sheet of the Dictionary had been taken to the printer, Andrew Millar, Johnson asked the messenger

DR JOHNSON AND OTHERS

what Millar had said: 'Sir (answered the messenger) he said, thank God I have done with him.' 'I am glad (replied Johnson, with a smile) that he thanks God for anything.'

For Johnson's second notable work of scholarship, both printers and readers had to put up with even longer delay. The formal *Proposals* for the edition of Shakespeare were published in 1756. With an optimism not uncommon amongst Shakespearian editors, Johnson promised that the work should be published by the end of 1757. In fact, it appeared in 1765. There was no list of subscribers. 'Sir', said Johnson, 'I have two very cogent reasons for not printing any list of subscribers;—one, that I have lost all the names,—the other, that I have spent all the money.' Here, indeed, was a mind cleared of cant. In 1908 Walter Raleigh wrote: 'Johnson's work on Shakespeare has not been superseded. He has been neglected and depreciated ever since the nineteenth century brought in the new aesthetic and philosophical criticism. The twentieth century, it seems likely, will treat him more respectfully.' This prophecy has been very precisely fulfilled: the latest of Shakespearian editors has not been ashamed to entitle the opening chapter of one of his books 'Back to Johnson'.

Apart from the details of Johnson's work as a textual and expository critic, the Preface to his Shakespeare is an illuminating expression of his approach to literature and the drama. One of his fundamental criticisms of Shakespeare was the criticism of the moral philosopher:

His precepts and axioms drop casually from him; he makes no just distribution of good and evil...he carries his persons indifferently through right and wrong and at the close dismisses them without further care, and leaves their examples to operate by chance. This fault the barbarity of his age cannot extenuate; for it is always a writer's duty to make the world better, and justice is a virtue independent on time and place.

'It is always a writer's duty to make the world better.' Taken out of its context the sentence might well be attributed to some Victorian copy-book. As such, it would be quickly and angrily controverted by those who maintain that it is a writer's primary duty as a literary artist to express himself; to determine what he wants to do and then to do it. To which Johnson, the moralist, would reply that what a writer wishes to do should be something which, directly or indirectly, should make for the amelioration of mankind. For to Johnson the world was very evil; for Johnson, above all men, as any reader of the *Prayers and Meditations* may discover, the times were always waxing late. This was a fundamental premise of his critical argument, but fortunately, cheerfulness broke in on occasion. He delighted in the character of the Nurse in *Romeo and Juliet*, although she was 'at once loquacious and secret, obsequious and insolent, trusty and dishonest'; Falstaff was a thief and a glutton, a coward and a boaster, but he was redeemed by the most pleasing of all qualities, perpetual gaiety; his licentiousness was not so offensive but that it might be borne for his mirth. There were, in short, worse ways of making the world better than by making it laugh.

Johnson's approach to the plays of Shakespeare, and to drama in general, is incorrigibly bookish. From his youth up he had been so deeply moved by the reading of Shakespeare, that he failed to appreciate the true function of the actor. An actor was a fellow who exhibited himself for a shilling, who clapped a hump on his back and a lump on his leg and cried 'I am Richard the Third'; many of Shakespeare's plays, he thought, were the worse for being acted.

Much of this depreciatory talk preserved by Boswell may be attributed to Johnson's desire to keep his old pupil, David Garrick, in his place. But behind it lay a view of the stage which cannot be accepted. 'The truth is', he wrote in the *Preface* to his edition of Shakespeare, 'that the spectators are always in their senses and know, from the first act to the last, that the stage is only a stage, and that the players are only players. They came to hear a certain number of lines recited with just gesture and elegant modulation.' Of the trials and uncertainties of the actor's life no one had a keener appreciation than Johnson, as the lines of his famous *Prologue* had shown:

> Ah! let not censure term our fate our choice;
> The stage, but echoes back the public voice;
> The drama's laws, the drama's patrons give,
> For we that live to please, must please to live.

But did Johnson really believe that the playgoer was satisfied by 'just gesture and elegant modulation'? Did he really believe that the actor was just a hireling who entertained by recitation? Was he really ignorant that the good actor ceases, for the time being, to be himself and gets into the very skin of the character that he is playing, that it is precisely by his power of making the audience forget everything except the play that the actor's quality must be judged?

We, too, 'must confess the faults of our favourite to gain credit to our praise of his excellencies'.

Johnson's pension had been awarded him by George III in 1762 and thereafter he regarded himself as emeritus. 'But I wonder, Sir', said Boswell, 'you have not more pleasure in writing than in not writing.' 'Sir', was the reply, 'you *may* wonder.' In fact what was destined to be the most popular, or more accurately, the least neglected of Johnson's writings, *The Lives of the Poets*, was published many years later. An introduction to a literary work was one of the things that Johnson was confident he could do very well, and he probably derived more pleasure from the actual writing of the *Lives* than of any other of his books. He even wrote at greater length than he need have done, being led on 'by the honest desire of giving useful pleasure'. The book-sellers increased his fee and Johnson was well content; 'The fact is', he said, 'not that they have paid me too little, but that I have written too much'—a view not commonly expressed by authors in their business negotiations.

The *Lives of the Poets* were the children of a comparatively happy old age; but the fame which Johnson had won through his earlier years of poverty and struggle rested upon his work as scholar and moralist rather than as literary critic. What served to spread his fame was his insatiable desire for company and conversation. Such moral principles and precepts as he had enunciated in his writings were not meant only for the study or the library or even the pulpit—they were meant for the dinner-table or the tavern chair. He was possessed of a mind, as Reynolds said, that was always ready for use and the company could listen to the application of the Rambler's philosophy to life as well as to literature, to politics as well as to morals, to business as well as to religion.

It is customary to describe Johnson as the great Tory of his century. Macaulay, of course, has a fine target: Johnson, he says, was a Tory 'not from rational conviction... but from mere passion.... The prejudices which he brought up to London were scarcely less absurd than those of his own Tom Tempest. Charles II and James II were two of the best kings that ever reigned.'

Of course Johnson's prejudices were on the side of monarchy; but he judged an individual monarch on his merits. When George III came to the throne, it seemed to him that it might be better if more power were entrusted to the crown and less to a group of corrupt or wrong-headed oligarchs. When Macaulay quotes his remarks about Charles II and James II he is referring to Johnson's retort when he had been deliberately provoked by Tom Davies. But in his *Introduction to the Political State of Great Britain*, written in 1756, Johnson wrote:

Thus the naval power of France continued to increase during the reign of Charles the Second, who, between his fondness of ease and pleasure, the struggles of faction, which he could not suppress, and his inclination to the friendship of absolute monarchy, had not much power or desire to repress it. And of James the Second it could not be expected that he should act against his neighbours with great vigour, having the whole body of his subjects to oppose. He was not ignorant of the real interest of his country; he desired its power and its happiness and thought rightly, that there is no happiness without religion; but he thought very erroneously and absurdly, that there is no religion without Popery.

Here is no monarchial passion, no idolatrous regard for the last two Stuart kings—merely a regret that the one had been pleasure-loving and the other fanatical. Johnson's passion was not for the monarchial principle, but for order, and it was the Whigs who seemed to him to be perpetually disturbing the ordered stability of government. The Devil was the first Whig, because he had upset the order of Paradise.

Leslie Stephen, in his great work on *English Thought in the Eighteenth Century*, devotes four pages to the Tories and, for all his admiration of the 'depth and massiveness' of Johnson's character, dismisses his political philosophy with frigid brevity. He quotes one paragraph from *Taxation no Tyranny*, in which Johnson asserts that there must in every society be some power from which there is no appeal, and concludes: 'That is Johnson's whole political theory.' But is the case so simple? Are the facts so clear? Leslie Stephen supports his conclusion by reference to Johnson's well-known utterances on Whigs and Whiggism—which he admits to be 'more or less humorous'—and declares that they embody his genuine creed. This is significant. Johnson's *obiter dicta* on the Whig party have indeed acquired a notoriety which tends to distort any genuine examination of his political opinions.

It is natural, but unfortunate, that an estimate of Johnson's political philosophy should commonly be based on his pamphlets, *Taxation no Tyranny* and *The False Alarm*. The first of these was an answer to the Resolutions of the American Congress of 1775. Johnson's case rested first upon the principle that 'the supreme power of every community has the right of requiring, from all its subjects, such contributions as are necessary to the publick safety or publick prosperity', and secondly upon his definition of a colony:

An English colony is a number of persons to whom the king grants a charter, permitting them to settle in some distant country and enabling them to constitute a corporation enjoying such powers as the charter grants, to be administered in such forms as the charter prescribes. As a corporation, they make laws for themselves; but as a corporation, subsisting by a grant from higher authority, to the control of authority they continue subject.

The colonists were, in Johnson's view, English subjects who had been allowed to reside abroad. They remained English subjects and enjoyed the protection of the armed forces of the crown against their enemies. For such protection it was equitable that they should pay. To the claim that there should be no taxation without representation, Johnson's reply was that the colonists had left the mother-country of their own accord and for their own purposes: 'He who goes voluntarily to America cannot complain of losing what he leaves in Europe. He, perhaps, had a right to vote for a knight or a burgess; by crossing the Atlantic, he has not nullified his right; but he has made its exertion no longer possible.'

It was, of course, a backward-looking view. Like some others of his own and later generations, Johnson looked upon colonists as naughty children who had run away from home. He would not recognise that they had grown up and begun to think for themselves.

The False Alarm was a protest against what a modern Whig historian has called 'the martyrdom and deification of the scandalous Wilkes'. Talk about Liberty in the abstract was always a source of irritation to Johnson, and when it was associated with a scoundrel (albeit a clubable scoundrel), his scorn was intensified. 'Every lover of liberty', he writes, 'stands doubtful of the fate of posterity, because the chief county in England cannot take its representative from a gaol.' *The False Alarm*, written in 1770, should be read alongside Boswell's description of his own greatest triumph, his reconciliation of Johnson and Wilkes at Mr Dilly's dinner-table six years later. There was nothing to equal it, said Edmund Burke, in the whole history of the Corps Diplomatique.

'The perpetual subject of political disquisition', wrote Johnson, 'is not absolute, but comparative good', and, in so far as he was prepared to accept any fundamental political postulates, his position was frequently as near that of John Locke as of any Tory philosopher. Quotations from Locke abound in the *Dictionary*, and in the preface which Johnson wrote to Dodsley's *Preceptor* Locke's works are specifically recommended. Locke had written a classical work on Toleration, and Johnson's views on this subject are recorded in more than one passage of Boswell:

Every society [he said] has a right to preserve publick peace and order and therefore has a good right to prohibit the propagation of opinions which have a dangerous tendency. To say the *magistrate* has this right, is using an inadequate word: it is the *society* for which the magistrate is agent.... Every man has a right to liberty of conscience and with that the magistrate cannot interefere.... But, Sir, no member of a society has a right to teach any doctrine contrary to what that society holds to be true.

Locke, arguing for the toleration of speculative opinions within any church, nevertheless declares that 'no opinions contrary to human society are to be tolerated by the magistrate', and his denial of toleration to the professed atheist was more categorical than any utterance of Johnson:

If we three [Johnson said once to Boswell and Seward] should discuss even the great question concerning the existence of a Supreme Being by ourselves, we should not be restrained;

for that would be to put an end to all improvement. But if we should discuss it in the presence of ten boarding-school girls, and as many boys, I think the magistrate would do well to put us in the stocks, to finish the debate there.

This is characteristic of Johnson's essentially practical view of moral and political problems. Fundamentally, he had as little interest in a system of political, as in one of metaphysical, philosophy. The famous lines which he contributed to Goldsmith's poem, *The Traveller*:

> How small of all that human hearts endure
> That part which kings or laws can cause or cure

are a characteristic epitome of his mistrust both of political theory and of political machinery. Locke's description of the state of nature may have seemed to Johnson to be conjectural and irrelevant, but when he made it clear that by the law of nature he meant a moral law derived from God, Johnson was more ready to listen to him. Politically, Johnson was no more an absolutist than Locke himself. 'There remains still in the people', wrote Locke, 'a supreme power to remove or alter the legislature', and it was a supremacy fully recognised by Johnson. When Sir Adam Fergusson emphasised the importance of keeping up a spirit in the people, so as to preserve a balance against the crown, Johnson was roused at once:

Why all this childish jealousy of the power of the crown? The crown has not power enough. When I say that all governments are alike, I consider that in no government power can be abused long. Mankind will not bear it. If a sovereign oppresses his people to a great degree they will rise and cut off his head. There is a remedy in human nature against tyranny, that will keep us safe under every form of government.

That is the core of Johnson's politics.

T. H. Green remarked that on Locke's theory of sovereignty it was impossible to pronounce when resistance to a *de facto* government is legitimate or otherwise and the same criticism might be made of Johnson. How is oppression 'to a great degree' to be defined? In another context Locke supplies his own answer: 'Who shall be the judge between them [the magistrate and his subjects]? I answer, God alone; for there is no judge upon earth between the supreme magistrate and the people'. Johnson might well have agreed in theory; in practice the common sense of humanity would decide when the time was ripe: 'mankind will not bear it'. Johnson, the traditional champion of established order, felt that there were many things which mankind ought not to bear. Slavery was one of them. *Taxation no Tyranny* has passed into the dreary limbo of political ephemera, but one sentence from it survives: 'How is it that we hear the loudest yelps for liberty among the drivers of negroes?' This was no mere debating point. In one of his earliest pieces of hackwork Johnson had asserted the natural right of the negroes to liberty and independence, and his care and affection for Francis Barber were something more than sentimental eccentricity.

Johnson's lack of sympathy with the claims and ambitions of colonists was, indeed, bound up with his misgivings about the treatment of native populations. Time after time he protested, like any nineteenth-century Radical, against the policy and practice of the invading conqueror. Reluctantly, he contrasted the English colonial governor unfavourably with his French counterpart:

A French governor is seldom chosen for any other reason than his qualifications for his trust. To be a bankrupt at home, or to be so infamously vicious that he cannot be decently protected in his own country, seldom recommends any man to the government of a French colony.... It is ridiculous to imagine that the friendship of nations, whether civil or barbarous, can be gained and kept but by kind treatment; and surely they who intrude, uncalled, upon the country of a distant people, ought to consider the natives as worthy of common kindness and content themselves to rob without insulting them.

Upon the Irish situation Johnson looked with dismay. 'The Irish', he declared in generous indignation, 'are in a most unnatural state; for we see there the minority prevailing over the majority', and, a little less seriously perhaps, he advised an Irishman: 'Do not make an union with us, Sir. We should unite with you, only to rob you', and of course he could not forbear to add: 'We should have robbed the Scotch if they had anything of which we could have robbed them.' In France, Johnson deplored the lack of healthy middle class between the magnificence of the rich and the misery of the poor; decent provision for the poor, he said, was the true test of civilisation.

On such great issues as those of war and peace Johnson was too large-minded to be uniformly consistent. In 1738 he had declaimed against Walpole's policy of appeasement; in 1771 he wrote one of his finest pamphlets in protest against a suggested war:

As war is the last of remedies, *cuncta prius tentanda*, all lawful expedients must be used to avoid it.... The life of a modern soldier is ill represented by heroick fiction. War has means of destruction more formidable than the cannon and the sword. Of the thousands and ten thousands that perished in our late contests with France and Spain, a very small part ever felt the stroke of an enemy; the rest languished in tents and ships, amidst damps and putrefaction; pale, torpid, spiritless and helpless, gasping and groaning, unpitied among men, made obdurate by long continuance of hopeless misery.... The wars of civilised nations make very slow changes in the system of empire. The publick perceives scarcely any alteration, but an increase of debt... at the conclusion of a ten years' war, how are we recompensed for the death of multitudes, and the expense of millions, but by contemplating the sudden glories of paymasters and agents, contractors and commissaries, whose equipages shine like meteors and whose palaces rise like exhalations.

Johnson could not know the horrors of total war. But in parenthesis one may recall his famous premonition of aerial assault: 'If men were all virtuous, I should with great alacrity teach them all to fly. But what would be the security of the good, if the bad could at pleasure invade them from the sky?... A flight of northern savages might hover in the wind and light at once with irresistible violence upon the capital of a fruitful region that was rolling under them.'

From all of which it would appear that it may be dangerous to accept without qualification the customary description of Johnson as the embodiment of eighteenth-century Toryism. The Rev. Dr Maxwell, sometime assistant Preacher of the Temple, wrote of him:

In politics he was deemed a Tory, but certainly was not so in the obnoxious or party sense of the term; for while he asserted the legal and salutary prerogatives of the crown, he no less respected the constitutional liberties of the people. Whiggism, at the time of the Revolution, he said, was accompanied with certain principles; but latterly, as a mere party distinction under Walpole and the Pelhams, was no better than the politicks of stock-jobbers and the religion of infidels.

The coupling of these two classes of society—stock-jobbers and infidels—is significant. Johnson's distrust of the Whig politician is closely akin to his distrust of the atheistic philosopher: both were lacking in moral principle, on the security of which depended the ordered happiness of human society. Locke's opinions might have been distorted by his followers, but his principles were fundamentally sound; Berkeley might have lost himself in a maze of metaphysical absurdity, but was a good man and a profound scholar. But Hume, by his intellectual arrogance, threatened to sap the foundations of human happiness, and as for Rousseau—he was simply the prophet of social and ethical anarchy and deserved to be sent to the plantations.

Clearly, Johnson's was not a master-mind in the sense that it inspired a school of philosophy or that it redirected the current of human thought. It was primarily a scholar's mind, which, having triumphed over 'toil, envy, want, the patron and the gaol', raised Johnson from the status of literary hack to the status of literary dictator; but it was also the mind of a Christian moralist. The elementary Christian doctrine of the sinfulness of man and of his redemption from the consequences of sin by the passion of Jesus Christ is implicit in all his writings as it is explicit in his *Prayers and Meditations*. Pleasures, as he said, were not necessarily vices, and Johnson's greatest pleasure was good talk at a good dinner-table. But what was his comment in his private meditations on that Holy Week of 1778?

> It has happened this week, as it never happened in Passion Week before, that I have never dined at home and I have therefore neither practised abstinence nor peculiar devotion.

On his seventieth birthday he prayed to God, in stark humility, that He would pardon the offences of seventy years and accept the remains of a misspent life. The philosophers might conceive of man as a political animal, but to Johnson he was primarily a creature possessed of a soul—and of a soul to be saved. Johnson was a stout champion of the freedom of the will, but what he would not, that he did. To assert the mastery of his fate or the captaincy of his soul would have seemed to him a mark not only of arrogance but of impiety. Man's highest faculty was his power of reasoning, but above and beyond Reason was a mist, as he wrote in *The Vision of Theodore*, which could be pierced only by the Eyes of Religion:

'I am Reason', declared the Nymph in that work, 'of all subordinate Beings the noblest and the greatest; who, if thou wilt receive my Laws, will reward thee like the rest of my Votaries, by conducting thee to Religion.'

When Goldsmith once remarked that the Club needed new members, since the existing members had already travelled over one another's minds, Johnson's reply was prompt and decisive: 'Sir, you have not travelled over *my* mind, I promise you.' *De nobis fabula narratur.* Such is the brilliance of the guide-book provided by James Boswell, that the exploration of Johnson's mind as revealed by his writings is frequently neglected.

One fact above all others is abundantly clear in Boswell's record—the personal mastery which Johnson, from his boyhood onwards, established over his fellows. 'No sooner did he arrive', writes Boswell of a dinner-party at Allan Ramsay's, 'than we were all as quiet as a school upon the entrance of the headmaster.' Johnson's range of reading was, of course, immense; but his intellectual and aesthetic limitations were notorious. He had little patience with purely speculative thought; he was blind to painting and deaf to music; he scorned the art of the actor. Yet neither Burke nor Reynolds, neither Burney nor Garrick had any hesitation in saluting him as master, whether at the Club or at any other social assembly.

In company Johnson's latent powers of wit and humour and even of pure fun were developed in a form that was seldom exhibited in his written work. For when he wrote, he was alone; and when he was alone, he was wretched.

In one of his rare autobiographical essays he writes of himself as Mr Sober: 'Mr Sober's chief leasure is conversation; there is no end of his talk or his attention; to speak or to hear is equally pleasing; for he still fancies that he is teaching or learning something, and is free for the time from his own reproaches. But there is one time at night when he must go home, that his friends may sleep....'

Men and women did not clamour to hear Johnson talk merely to enjoy the flash of repartee or the establishment of a debating point. In his talk, as in his writing, there was an oracular quality, and when Mrs Thrale, in compiling her famous mark-sheet, gave Johnson full marks (20) for Religion, Morality, and General Knowledge, 19 for Scholarship, 16 for Humour, 15 for Wit, and nothing at all for Person and Voice, Manners, or Good Humour, her judgment was shrewd and her awards at least as accurate as those of most examiners. Johnson's hearers did not fancy that they were learning something —they were convinced of it. And their conviction sprang not only from the wealth of Johnson's knowledge or from the vigour of his exposition, but from the passionate sincerity of his search for wisdom and truth and goodness.

It was left for Boswell to adorn the tale; it was Johnson who pointed the moral.

2. *THE CHURCHMAN*

In Overton and Relton's work on *The English Church from the Accession of George I to the End of the Eighteenth Century* two pages are devoted to a sketch of Samuel Johnson as a Churchman. From them the following passages may be quoted:

> He is even a more valuable witness to the good qualities of the Church of his day than Edmund Burke, for he was more of a representative man. His manliness and robustness of intellect, his strong common-sense, his firm and unwavering conviction of the truth of Christianity, combined with a vivid interest in the affairs of this life, his sturdy independence both of thought and action, his real piety without a tincture of cant or 'enthusiasm' were all characteristic of the eighteenth century at its best....
>
> He was not bound to the Church by any ties. His attachment to it was purely one of conviction and all the more valuable on that account....
>
> The eighteenth-century church arrangements quite satisfied him. He was very comfortable in his seat in St Clement Danes, and the somewhat secular character of his clerical friend, Dr Taylor, does not seem at all to have shocked him.... Johnson's devotional writings...show him to have been a man of profound personal religious character and conviction, deeply attached to his personal Saviour....

It is a pleasant, cosy picture—and profoundly misleading. By way of commentary, it may be well, in the first instance, to recall very briefly the background of his birth and boyhood.

Johnson was born over his father's book-shop at the corner of the market-place at Lichfield. Across the cobbles was St Mary's Church in which he was baptised. His father, Michael Johnson, though not prosperous as a bookseller, was a prominent citizen, serving as sheriff, magistrate, and senior bailiff. Politically, or at least sentimentally, he was a Jacobite and a High Churchman, but in common with other holders of office in the city he regularly abjured the Pretender and subscribed to the declaration that there was not any transubstantiation in the Sacrament of the Lord's Supper. He worshipped regularly at St Mary's. Johnson's mother, on the other hand, came from an evangelical family and it was from her that at the age of three he received his first introduction to theological dogma:

> Being in bed with my mother one morning, I was told by her of the two places to which the inhabitants of this world were received after death; one a fine place filled with happiness, called Heaven; the other a *sad* place, called Hell.

It was a warning which Johnson never forgot. Meanwhile, at about the age of nine he was troubled by doubts and became a lax talker against religion. His mother gave him *The Whole Duty of Man* to read on Sundays, but it brought him no conviction; Grotius' *de Veritate Religionis*, which he picked up in his father's shop, was too difficult for him; but Law's *Serious Call*, which he read at Oxford, had a totally different effect. He expected to find it dull or even ludicrous. On the contrary, it was, in his own words, 'quite an overmatch for him', and from that time forward religion, as Boswell says, was 'the predominant object of his thoughts'.

DR JOHNSON THE CHURCHMAN

It is one of Boswell's merits that he gives us the gloomy, as well as the gay, side of Johnson's temperament and, whatever may be thought of Boswell's morals, his interest in, and his desire for, a stable religious faith were genuine. In particular, he frequently asked Johnson to arm him with a concise apologetic. 'Sir,' was the reply, 'you cannot answer all objections'; and then he went on to say that while it might be demonstrated that the First Cause was good as well as powerful, there stood over against it the unhappiness of human life. It was only 'a positive revelation' which had made it possible to hope for a future state of compensation and a perfect system.

It was seldom, indeed, that the introduction of a religious topic did not lead Johnson to the contemplation of death and the judgment it would bring. Boswell's account of the dinner-party at Mr Dilly's on 15 April 1778, already quoted,[1] includes a long argument with Mrs Knowles, the Quakeress:

MRS KNOWLES 'The Scriptures tell us "The righteous shall have *hope* in his death".' JOHNSON 'Yes, Madam; that is, he shall not have despair. But, consider, his hope of salvation must be founded on the terms on which it is promised that the mediation of our Saviour shall be applied to us—namely, obedience; and where obedience has failed, then, as suppletory to it, repentance. But what man can say that his obedience has been such, as he would approve of in another, or even in himself upon close examination, or that his repentance has not been such as to require being repeated of? No man can be sure that his obedience and repentance will obtain salvation.' MRS KNOWLES 'But divine intimation of acceptance may be made to the soul.' JOHNSON 'Madam, it may; but I should not think the better of a man who should tell me on his death-bed

[1] See pp. 41, 42.

he was sure of salvation. A man cannot be sure himself that he has divine intimation of acceptance; much less can he make others sure that he has it.' BOSWELL 'Then, Sir, we must be contented to acknowledge that death is a terrible thing.' JOHNSON 'Yes, Sir. I have made no approaches to a state which can look on it as not terrible.' MRS KNOWLES (seeming to enjoy a pleasing serenity in the persuasion of benignant divine light) 'Does not St Paul say "I have fought the good fight of faith, I have finished my course; henceforth is laid up for me a crown of life"?' JOHNSON 'Yes, madam; but here was a man inspired, a man who had been converted by supernatural interposition.' BOSWELL 'In prospect death is dreadful; but in fact we find that people die easy.' JOHNSON 'Why, Sir, most people have not *thought* much of the matter, so cannot *say* much, and it is supposed they die easy. Few believe it certain they are then to die; and those who do, set themselves to behave with resolution, as a man does who is going to be hanged. He is not the less unwilling to be hanged.' MISS SEWARD 'There is one mode of the fear of death which is certainly absurd; and that is the dread of annihilation, which is only a pleasing sleep without a dream.' JOHNSON 'It is neither pleasing, nor sleep; it is nothing....'

More and more, as he grew older, Johnson was disturbed by this apprehension of annihilation. Some people, he said, looked upon salvation as the effect of an absolute decree: Others, and those the most rational, looked upon salvation as conditional. 'And those the most rational.' Here we come near to the heart of Johnson's mental agony. His reason told him that the sinner must be punished. His religion told him that sinners could be saved by the sacrifice which Christ had made for the sins of the whole world. But what of the sinner himself? Johnson could not throw himself in an airy optimism upon the mercy of God. He had conditions to fulfil—obedience, repentance, reformation. Conscious that he had not fulfilled them, he was afraid. So when the amiable Dr Adams, the Master of his old college, suggested that God was infinitely good, Johnson agreed, but feared that not having fulfilled the conditions of salvation he might be one of those who would be damned. 'DR ADAMS "What do you mean by damned?" JOHNSON (passionately and loudly) "Sent to Hell, Sir, and punished everlastingly."'

Apart from Boswell's testimony, Johnson's recurrent anxiety about the problems of sin and salvation is evident in his *Prayers and Meditations*, posthumously published in 1785. In the catalogue of his sins Johnson emphasised sensual thoughts, idleness, late rising, neglect of Bible-reading, and irregularity in public worship. Year after year he recorded his shortcomings, his failure to keep his resolutions of a year ago, his determination to do better in the future. On Easter Eve 1761, for instance, he wrote:

> Since the communion of last Easter, I have led a life so dissipated and useless and my terrours and perplexities have so much increased, that I am under great depression and discouragement; yet I purpose to present myself before God tomorrow, with humble hope that He will not break the bruised reed.
>
> *Come unto me, all ye that travail*
>
> I have resolved (I hope not presumptuously) till I am afraid to resolve again. Yet, hoping in God, I steadfastly purpose to lead a new life. O God, enable me, for Jesus Christ's sake.

And then follows the regular list of resolutions.

'O God,' he prayed at another time, 'make me to remember that the night cometh when no man can work.' Always he reflected on the fact that his love of good talk at a good dinner-table had stolen the hours that should have been spent in methodical study. Our chief delight in Johnson comes, of course, from the record of these stolen hours and we tend to forget that for Johnson life was an unending struggle. It was at the Mitre or at the Club, not in St Clement Danes Church, that he was truly comfortable. Did he not describe a tavern chair as the throne of human felicity? But when he returned to the solitude of his study, he wrote:

> To strive with difficulties and to conquer them is the highest human felicity; the next is, to strive and deserve to conquer; but he whose life has passed without a contest and who can boast neither success nor merit, can survey himself only as a useless filler of existence; and if he is content with his own character, must owe his satisfaction to insensibility.

This is the true Johnson—*Johnson Agonistes*, to quote the title of the most penetrating essay of recent years.[1]

To modern readers, as they contemplate the *Dictionary of the English Language* and the dozen volumes of *Collected Works*, Johnson's doubts and fears and discontents may well suggest the morbidity of a spiritual hypochondriac. But Johnson had inherited a vile melancholy from his father and a certain element of Calvinism from his mother, and his preoccupation with his sin of slothfulness was constant and fundamental. Religion was for him the only alternative to despair, but it brought him no easy comfort. Speaking of one of Hugh Blair's Sermons, of which he had a profound admiration, he remarked: 'There is one part of it which I disapprove, and I'd have him correct it; which is, that "he who does not feel joy in religion is far from the kingdom of heaven!" There are many good men whose fear of God predominates over their love.'

[1] B. H. Bronson, *Johnson Agonistes and other Essays* (Cambridge, 1946).

Johnson was one of those good men. He feared God not perhaps as a criminal might fear the sentence of an implacable judge, but as a wayward and lazy sixth-form boy might fear the end-of-term interviews with his headmaster. He praised Law's *Serious Call* as the finest piece of hortatory theology in the language, but such a comment as that of Law that 'the innocent Christ did not suffer to quiet an angry Deity, but as co-operating, assisting and uniting with that love of God which desired our salvation' seems to have brought him little comfort. On the other hand, the divine who gave him most satisfaction was the heterodox Samuel Clarke, in spite of the fact that he felt bound to exclude him from the *Dictionary* on account of his Arian views. But he frequently read and commended his preaching. Clarke's sermons fill ten substantial volumes, and without making too arbitrary a choice one may conjecture that a passage such as the following from a sermon *Of the Love of God towards Sinners* may have renewed Johnson's hopes:

> Most unjustly therefore and with great injury to Religion, is God sometimes represented as an implacable and cruel Judge, delighting in the destruction of Sinners, till they were taken (as it were) out of his Hands by the Interposition of Christ; This (I say) is a very injurious Representation of the Great God and Father of Mercies: For, the Coming of Christ was not the first Cause of the Goodness and Love of God towards us; but the essential and eternal Goodness of God was the cause and reason of the Coming of Christ.

On his death-bed, happily, Johnson's fears were calmed by 'the prevalence of his faith, and his trust in the merits and *propitiation* of Jesus Christ'. He urged his doctor to read Clarke's sermons, and when he was asked why he thus pressed the work of an Arian, he replied: 'Because he is fullest on the *propitiatory sacrifice.*'

So much for the gloomier side of Johnson's theology. But even Johnson realised, on occasions, that cheerfulness was a religious virtue. It is pleasant to believe that it was not an accident that on Easter Day 1778, two days after Oliver Edwards had made his immortal remark about cheerfulness breaking in, Johnson added to his usual Easter resolutions: 'To serve and trust God and be cheerful.' It is refreshing, too, to note that occasionally he revolted from the contemplation of death and judgment. When Boswell once pressed him with the question 'May we not fortify our minds for the approach of death?', he broke out angrily: 'No, sir, let it alone. It matters not how a man dies, but how he lives', and certainly no one of his own or any other age practised the virtue of Christian charity more consistently than Johnson.

As a Churchman, Johnson never wavered in his allegiance to the Establishment. His insistence on the need for an ordered society, which Macaulay misinterpreted as 'mere passion',[1] made him distrust the Methodists as he distrusted the Whigs. But in his religion, as in his politics, there was plenty of liberal thinking. Within certain limits he could appreciate the qualities of a Quaker or a Methodist. He enjoyed the conversation of Wesley (though he deplored that he was 'always obliged to go at a certain hour') and gave Boswell a letter of introduction to him because he thought it 'very much to be wished that worthy and religious men should be acquainted with each other'; he believed that Whitefield did good, but added that he knew him before he began to be better than other

[1] See p. 58.

people. In his *Dictionary* he had defined *Enthusiast* as 'one who vainly imagines a private revelation' and it was the claim of the Methodists to the 'inward light' which irritated him: 'If a man pretends to a principle of action of which I can know nothing...how can I tell what that person may be prompted to do? When a person professes to be governed by a written ascertained law, I can then know where to find him.' Similarly, while he could admire and enjoy a Presbyterian sermon, he deplored the lack of an ordered liturgy:

'Why, Sir, the Presbyterians have no church, no apostolical ordination.' BOSWELL 'And do you think that absolutely essential, Sir?' JOHNSON 'Why, Sir, as it was an apostolical institution, I think it is dangerous to be without it. And, Sir, Presbyterians have no publick worship; they have no form of prayer in which they know they are to join. They go to hear a man pray and are to judge whether they will join with him.'

Furthermore, the Presbyterians paid no regard to festivals:

I am sorry to have it to say, that Scotland is the only Christian country, Catholick or Protestant, where the great events of our religion are not solemnly commemorated by its ecclesiastical establishment, on days set apart for the purpose.

When Johnson was in Sir Robert Chambers' garden in Oxford and Sir Robert was gathering snails and throwing them over the wall into his neighbour's garden, Johnson reproached him very roughly for being unmannerly and unneighbourly. 'Sir,' said Sir Robert, 'my neighbour is a Dissenter.' 'Oh,' said Johnson, 'if so, Chambers, toss away, toss away....'

Towards the Church of Rome Johnson was more

sympathetic. 'A good man,' he said, 'of a timorous disposition, in great doubt of his acceptance with God, and pretty credulous, might be glad of a church where there are so many helps to get to Heaven. I would be a Papist if I could. I have fear enough; but an obstinate rationality prevents me.' Here again, it is *Johnson Agonistes* who speaks.

As to particular Catholic doctrines, he was willing to attack or defend them according to his mood and the circumstances of the argument. He was prepared to support the doctrine of Purgatory but condemned the 'lucrative imposition' to which it led in practice. He denied that the Mass was 'idolatrous' but regarded the giving of the sacrament in one kind as criminal. In short he concluded: 'In everything in which they differ from us they are wrong.'

'A steady Church of England man.' Such is Boswell's description of Johnson. It might have been more accurate to call him 'a steady Prayer Book man'. When he was still in petticoats Johnson was told by his mother to learn the Gospel for the day by heart. This he did in a few minutes, and throughout his life the Book of Common Prayer was the principal source of his religious instruction and refreshment. 'I know of no good prayers but those in the Book of Common Prayer', he said, and in his own compositions the influence of the book is evident. His very last poem, written eight days before his death, was a paraphrase in Latin elegiacs of the collect of the Communion service, beginning '*Summe Deus cui caeca patent penetralia cordis*....' The Prayer Book, in fact, was the mainspring of his meditation and his worship. He went to church on Sundays with reasonable regularity and if he missed a Sunday, he tried to make it up in the week. In general, he worshipped more frequently when there were prayers only and not a sermon—not that he despised sermons, but he had written a good many himself and he was an exacting critic.

For the office of clergyman he had the highest respect, so high that when he was invited to take Holy Orders and accept a country living in the gift of his friend Bennet Langton, he had scruples which he could not overcome. 'I have not,' he said, 'the requisites for the office and I cannot, in my conscience, shear that flock which I am unable to feed.' Having so high a respect for the clergy, he demanded a high standard of seemly behaviour and also of seemly dress. From bishops he expected the very highest degree of decorum, and an episcopal invitation to dinner in Holy Week put him into a serious state of embarrassment; his bow to an Archbishop was described as 'such a studied elaboration of homage, such an extension of limb, such a flexion of body as have seldom or never been equalled'. His sense of fun was, of course, far too keen for him to deny to the clergy the pleasure of a joke. What he hated was a clergyman who assumed the 'lax jollity' of a man of the world. It was this that provoked his famous comment: 'This merriment of parsons is mighty offensive.' Similarly, for all his affection for, and gratitude towards, his old friend Dr Taylor, he deplored the way in which the Squire in Taylor tended to predominate over the Parson, 'Sir, I love him... but my regard for him does not increase... His talk is of bullocks ... His habits are by no means sufficiently clerical.'

To Anglicans of today Johnson's habit of partaking of the Holy Communion only once a year may seem strange.

One might expect that he would have attended at each of the great festivals of the Church, and late in life one of his resolves was 'participation of the Sacrament at least three times a year'. But his *Prayers and Meditations* show clearly how agonizing was his mental preparation, combined with fasting and the reading of Clarke's sermons, for his Easter communion. 'By this awful festival,' he wrote at the age of seventy-one, 'is particularly recommended newness of life; and a new life I will now endeavour to begin, by more diligent application to useful employment and more frequent attendance on public worship.' Johnson wrote many sermons for Dr Taylor and from one of them (on the text 'But let a man examine himself, and so let him eat of that bread and drink of that cup') we may get a clear picture of his considered view of the meaning of the Sacrament:

> This sacrament is a representation of the death of our Saviour, appointed by himself, to be celebrated by all his followers, in all ages; to the end that by commemorating his sufferings in a solemn and public manner, they might declare their confidence in his merits, their belief of his mission, and their adherence to his religion.... By partaking of the communion, we declare, in the most solemn manner, in the presence of God and man, that we hold the faith of Jesus.... We are therefore not transiently and carelessly, but frequently and seriously, to ask ourselves whether we firmly believe the promises of our Saviour—whether we repent of our sins—and resolve, for the future, to avoid all those things which God has forbidden and practise all those which he has commanded. And when any man is convinced that he has formed real resolutions of a new life, let him pray for strength and constancy to persevere in them; and let him come joyfully to the holy table, in sure confidence of pardon, reconciliation, and life everlasting.

'Not transiently and carelessly'—here is the explanation of the infrequency of Johnson's participation in the Sacrament. Here, too, is evidence that in the last analysis Johnson's mind and conscience were concentrated not on the doctrines of a particular Church but on the central facts of the Christian religion. For all his prejudices, his intolerance in argument, and his devotion to the Anglican liturgy, Johnson never magnified the ultimate importance of forms of worship, of ceremonial, or of vesture. Believing, as he did, that all Christians agreed on the essential articles of the faith, he displayed some impatience, for instance, at the Puritan and Quaker arguments against 'showy decorations of the human figure':

> Oh let us not be found when our Master calls us, ripping the lace off our waistcoats, but the spirit of contention from our souls and tongues... a man who cannot get to heaven in a green coat, will not find his way thither the sooner in a grey one.

When his own time came, he strove to practise what he had preached. Having been told by his doctor, in answer to a plain question, that without a miracle he could not recover, 'Then', he said, 'I will take no more physick, not even my opiates; for I have prayed that I may render up my soul to God unclouded.' In death, as in life, he cleared his mind of cant.

3. *THE BIOGRAPHER*

Few would quarrel with Walter Raleigh's description of *The Lives of the Poets* as the most memorable of Johnson's literary works; and even those readers who are bored by *Rasselas* and *The Rambler* still derive genuine pleasure from the wealth of wit and anecdotal criticism in which

DR JOHNSON AND OTHERS

the *Lives* abound. In the opening sentence of the *Life* Boswell described Johnson as one who 'excelled all mankind in writing the lives of others', and it may be worth while to recall how large biography loomed in his earliest apprenticeship to journalism.

When Johnson arrived in London in 1737 with $2\frac{1}{2}d.$ in his pocket, he was fully conscious that he must earn his living by his pen and one of his earliest proposals to Edward Cave was for a translation of Father Paul Sarpi's *History of the Council of Trent*. Cave accepted the proposal and, what was more important from Johnson's point of view, agreed to pay for the work by instalments as the copy came in. Characteristically, Johnson fell behind the appointed dates; but he had other things to do and wrote a spirited reply to Cave's complaint: 'If you find the progress hereafter not such as you have a right to expect, you can easily stimulate a negligent translator.' In fact the work was never published, since by an extraordinary coincidence another Mr (John) Johnson, curate of St Martin-in-the-Fields was engaged upon the same laborious task. In the end, as Boswell puts it, the two Johnsons destroyed each other, for neither of them went on with the work. Meanwhile, in *The Gentleman's Magazine* for November 1738, Samuel Johnson had written a short *Life* of Father Paul Sarpi and thus his first formal essay in biography was a preliminary advertisement of a forthcoming work. It was brief and pertinent. The character and career of Father Paul are concisely summarised and full weight is given to the great part he played in the struggle between Pope Paul V and the Republic of Venice. When Venice was laid under an interdict, Father Paul became the champion of national freedom against Papal aggression. On such a topic Johnson was not likely to display an anaemic impartiality and even in a short biographical essay he found room to express his scorn of Papal claims:

> The propositions [he writes] maintained on the side of Rome were these: That the Pope is invested with all the authority of heaven and earth....That the Pope cannot err...that the Pope is God upon earth...that to call *his* power in question, is to call in question the power of God: maxims equally shocking, weak, pernicious, and absurd! which did not require the abilities or learning of Father Paul to demonstrate their falsehood....

There speaks the stout Anglican and at the end of the essay he makes a further point:

> He [Father Paul] appears by many passages of his life to have had a high esteem of the church of England; and his friend, Father Fulgentio, who had adopted all his notions, made no scruple of administering to Dr Duncombe, an English gentleman that fell sick at Venice, the communion in both kinds, according to the Common Prayer which he had with him in Italian.

Johnson's second essay in biography was topical. Hermann Boerhaave, Professor at the University at Leyden and one of the most famous physicians of the eighteenth century, had died in 1738. Johnson's interest in physic was, at least, as lively as his interest in ecclesiastical politics; a memorial oration delivered at Leyden gave him the facts he needed for a series of articles in *The Gentleman's Magazine* for 1739 and he wrote *con amore* of a man who 'formed the design of gaining a complete knowledge of medicine by way of digression from theological studies'. In this and other pieces Johnson made no pretence of original investigation. He was writing magazine articles of topical interest. Of the stories of Boerhaave's remarkable powers of diagnosis he writes:

> I mention none of them, because I have no opportunity of collecting testimonies, or distinguishing between those accounts which are well proved, and those which owe their rise to fiction and credulity.

What appealed to Johnson in Boerhaave was his piety ('He asserted on all occasions the divine authority and sacred efficacy of the holy scriptures') and the thoroughness of his scientific work ('He examined the observations of other men, but trusted only to his own'). Already Johnson knew enough of the scholar's life to realise the steady labour it involved. 'Statesmen and generals', he wrote 'may grow great by unexpected accidents and a fortunate concurrence of circumstances, neither procured nor foreseen by themselves: but reputation in the learned world must be the effect of industry and capacity.'

Edward Cave was no doubt satisfied with these first samples of his contributor's biographical work; for in the following year (1740) he commissioned lives of Admiral Blake, Sir Francis Drake, and John Philip Barretier.

In 1740 England was at war with Spain—'an enemy' in Johnsons' view, 'whose insults, ravages and barbarities had long called for vengeance'. This was a sentiment which had been expressed with some vigour in *London* two years before and in compiling his 'succinct narration' of the life and actions of Admiral Blake, Johnson had 'nothing farther in view than to do justice to his bravery and conduct without intending any parallel between his achievement and those of our present admirals'.

Again, Johnson makes no claim to originality. His *Life* of Blake was, in fact, a paraphrase of an anonymous work in a series of *Lives English and Foreign* published in 1704, and when he sums up Blake's moral character he frankly quotes the estimate given in that work. One remark of Blake's which Johnson recalls no doubt gave him special satisfaction: 'It is not the business of a seaman to mind state-affairs, but to hinder foreigners from fooling us.'

The *Life* of Sir Francis Drake was a much longer piece, appearing in five successive instalments in *The Gentleman's Magazine*. As the bibliographers are careful to point out, it has little intrinsic value. But here and there Johnson was led to characteristic reflections upon topics of general interest. About the natives for instance, of a South American Kingdom conquered by Drake, he wrote:

Whether more enlightened nations ought to look upon them with pity, as less happy than themselves, some sceptics have made, very unnecessarily, a difficulty of determining. More, they say, is lost by the perplexities than gained by the instruction of science; we enlarge our vices with our knowledge and multiply our wants with our attainments, and the happiness of life is better secured by the ignorance of vice than by the knowledge of virtue.

This, says Johnson, is a fallacious presentation of the problem:

The question is [he goes on] not whether a good Indian or bad Englishman be most happy; but which state is most desirable, supposing virtue and reason the same in both.

Nor is this the only mistake which is generally admitted in this controversy, for these reasoners frequently confound innocence with the mere incapacity of guilt. He that never saw, or heard, or thought of strong liquors, cannot be proposed as a pattern of sobriety.

Here is no paraphrase of earlier writers. It is *The Rambler* in embryo.

Johnson had a horror of the sea and of the sailor's life and there is a touch of irony in his absorption in the lives of famous admirals, but the business of these admirals was to 'hinder foreigners from fooling us' and, writing in 1740, Johnson could take some pleasure in recording the discomfiture of Spaniards.

From admirals he turned, or was directed, to scholars. About the composition of his essay on John Philip Barretier he is perfectly frank:

> Having not been able to procure materials for a compleat life of Mr Barretier, and being nevertheless willing to gratify the curiosity justly raised in the public by his uncommon attainments, we think the following extracts of letters, written by his father, proper to be inserted in our collection.

And then follows an account of youthful precocity as depressing as that recorded in the autobiography of John Stuart Mill: Barretier at the age of nine years was master of five languages; at eleven he published a learned letter in Latin and translated the travels of Rabbi Benjamin from Hebrew into French; in his twelfth year he applied himself to patristic studies, reading every author in the original since he had formed a profound mistrust of translators; at the age of fifteen he published a theological treatise on St John's Gospel which was of such quality that 'not only the publick, but princes, who are commonly the last by whom merit is distinguished, began to interest themselves in his success'. At the University of Halle the professors were so much impressed by his conversation that they immediately offered him a Ph.D. That same night the young man produced a thesis on mathematical philosophy which on the following day he defended amid the acclamations of the whole university. At Berlin the King of Prussia endeavoured to interest him in the study of modern history and 'of those parts of learning that are of use in publick transactions'; but the young man was not prepared to desert his private studies for 'such harassing fatigues'. Later, he was prevailed upon to enlarge his range and at the University of Halle continued 'to increase his reputation by new performances'. But, alas, his health began to decline and at the age of twenty he died. *Sic transit gloria studiorum.* Perhaps Johnson had him in mind when he wrote *The Vanity of Human Wishes*. That he took more than a passing interest in Barretier's carrer is shown by the additional pages he contributed to *The Gentleman's Magazine* in 1742 and by the separate publication of the *Life* in the form of a sixpenny pamphlet in 1744. For this the text was revised and augmented, particularly in relation to Barretier's way of life:

> With regard to common Life, he had some peculiarities. He could not bear Musick, and if he was ever engaged at Play, could not attend to it. He neither loved Wine nor Entertainments, nor Dancing, nor the Sports of the Field, nor relieved his studies with any other Diversion than that of Walking and Conversation. He eat little Flesh and lived almost wholly upon Milk, Tea, Bread, Fruits and Sweetmeats.

Of the other *Lives* written by Johnson at this period, that of Morin, the French botanist, was a translation of the *éloge* by Fontenelle; in writing the *Life* of Peter Burman, the Dutch classical scholar, he was faced with another youthful prodigy who qualified for admission to the University of Utrecht at the age of thirteen. This was a little too much for Johnson to swallow:

> To reduce this narrative to credibility [he writes] it is necessary that admiration should give place to inquiry and that it be discovered what proficiency in literature is expected from a student, requesting to be admitted into a Dutch university.

and he goes on to explain that a freshman at Utrecht was not as proficient in languages or composition as a boy in the higher classes of an English school. But Johnson had a high regard for Burman's scholarship. A man who produced good editions of Quintilian, Valerius Flaccus and Ovid was a man after his own heart and he specially commended his behaviour on receiving his doctorate at the age of twenty.

> The attainment of this honour was far from having upon Burman that effect which has been too often observed to be produced in others, who, having in their own opinion no higher object of ambition, have elapsed into idleness and security, and spent the rest of their lives in a lazy enjoyment of their academical dignities.

In this oblique criticism of eighteenth-century dons Johnson seems, for once, to be in accord with Gibbon.

The last of Johnson's biographical essays belonging to these early years was the *Life* of Dr Thomas Sydenham (1624-89) printed in *The Gentleman's Magazine* in 1742 and prefixed to the new translation of Sydenham's works by John Swan.

Johnson was always happy in writing about physic and physicians. Sydenham, who came to be known as the English Hippocrates, was at once a notable writer on, and a notable victim of, the gout and his treatise on that subject is one of the most celebrated of his works. Johnson duly notes that after taking an M.B. degree at Oxford and holding a fellowship at All Souls he became an M.D. of Cambridge. Regrettably, he omits the fact that he took the degree after being admitted to membership of Pembroke College.

Such, in brief, were Johnson's preliminary excursions in biographical composition and he was under no illusion about their quality or their importance. They were straightforward, readable summaries of the careers of various men which, in Cave's judgment, would be of interest to the readers of *The Gentleman's Magazine*. They were frankly based on secondary sources and are an early illustration of Johnson's skill in 'tearing the heart out of a book'. As he wrote in *The Rambler*, no. 145:

> These papers of the day, the ephemerae of learning, have uses more adequate to the purposes of common life than more pompous and durable volumes.... Even the abridger, compiler and translator, though their labours cannot be ranked with those of the diurnal historiographer, yet must not be rashly doomed to annihilation. Every size of readers requires a genius of correspondent capacity.

But in 1744 Johnson produced a biography that was more than a compilation or an abridgment. He wrote the *Life* of a friend who died in the preceding year—Richard Savage. This was something very different from the ephemerae of learning. It was Johnson's first biographical work of any importance. It was also the first important contribution to a subject which now has a substantial bibliography of its own.

The story of Sir Joshua Reynolds picking up the book

and beginning to read it with his arm leaning against a chimney-piece is well known: 'It seized his attention so strongly, that, not being able to lay down the book till he had finished it, when he attempted to move, he found his arm totally benumbed.' If a modern reader should fail to re-enact Sir Joshua's absorption, he should remember the vibrant topicality of the subject in 1744. Savage died on 1 August 1743. In *The Gentleman's Magazine* for that month, Johnson addressed an anonymous letter to the editor, intreating him to inform the publick that a life of Savage would speedily be published by 'a person who was favoured with his confidence'. Johnson was well aware of what today would be called the 'news-value' of Savage's career and he was anxious to stake a claim, not with a view to his own literary advancement (for the *Life*, like the letter, was to be anonymous), but in order that the story of Richard Savage should be truthfully told:

It may be reasonably imagined [he wrote] that others may have the same design; but as it is not credible that they can obtain the same materials, it must be expected they will supply from invention the want of intelligence; and that under the title of 'The Life of Savage' they will publish only a novel, filled with romantick adventures and imaginary amours. You may, therefore, perhaps, gratify the lovers of truth and wit, by giving me leave to inform them in your Magazine, that my account will be published in 8vo by Mr Roberts in Warwick Lane.

Having thus committed himself, Johnson was not inhibited by his customary procrastination; he sat up all night and wrote forty-eight octavo pages at a sitting. His first-hand knowledge was confined to the last six years of Savage's life and the latest and most scholarly biographer of Savage[1] points out that for the earlier periods Johnson, relying on previously printed accounts and on unverified anecdote, failed to establish an accurate chronology. But Johnson was not engaged upon a definitive biography; he was concerned that the first tribute to Savage after his death should be the tribute of a friend and he had not time to verify his references.

The mystery of Richard Savage, like the mystery of Edwin Drood, will never be solved; but whatever may be the truth about his birth, his career is one of the many examples of the truths that are stranger than fiction.

His claim to be the illegitimate son of Lord Rivers and the Countess of Macclesfield; the bitter enmity of his mother; his struggles as an author; his fantastic extravagance; his conviction for murder in a tavern brawl and his subsequent reprieve; his disappointment at not being made Poet Laureate and his self-appointment as 'Volunteer Laureat' to Queen Caroline; his banishment to South Wales and his death at a relatively early age in a debtor's prison in Bristol; here, as Johnson perceived, was abundant material for romance.

Johnson prophesied better than he knew about the novelists. Charles Whitehead's *Richard Savage: A Romance of Real Life* was published in 1842 and reissued in 1896; J. M. Barrie's first play, written in collaboration with H. B. Marriott Watson, was *Richard Savage* produced, with a prologue by W. E. Henley, in 1891; yet another romantic biography was S. V. Makower's *Richard Savage: A Mystery in Biography* (1909), and later came Gwyn Jones's novel *Richard Savage* (1935).

[1] C. Tracy, *The Artificial Bastard, A Biography of Richard Savage*, (Toronto, 1953).

But it is time to return to Johnson as biographer and in the opening paragraphs we are bidden to 'mark what ills the scholar's life assail':

> The Heroes of literary as well as civil History have been very often no less remarkable for what they have suffered, than for what they have achieved; and Volumes have been written only to enumerate the Miseries of the Learned, and relate their unhappy Lives, and untimely Deaths.
>
> To these mournful Narratives, I am about to add the Life of *Richard Savage*, a Man whose Writings entitle him to an eminent Rank in the Classes of Learning, and whose Misfortunes claim a Degree of Compassion, not always due to the Unhappy, as they were often the Consequences of the Crimes of others, rather than his own.

Thus Johnson makes no claim to a frigid impartiality. He accepted what Savage had told him, and what others had written, of Savage's early career and went on to write of the man he had known since his own arrival in London in 1737.

> Born with a legal Claim to Honour and to Riches [he writes] he was in two months illegitimated by the Parliament, and disowned by his Mother; doomed to Poverty and Obscurity, and launched upon the Ocean of Life, only that he might be swallowed by its Quicksands, or dashed upon its Rocks.

Then follows the account of his schooling at a small Grammar School, his deprivation by his mother of the legacy left to him by his father, his unsuccessful writing of comedies, his short-lived friendship with Steele, his playing of the title-role in his own tragedy *Sir Thomas Overbury*. Johnson gives a vivid picture of Savage while he was writing the play:

> During a considerable Part of the Time...he was without Lodging, and often without Meat; nor had he any other Con-

veniences for Study than the Fields or the Streets allowed him, there he used to walk and form his Speeches, and afterwards step into a Shop, beg for a few moments the Use of the Pen and Ink, and write down what he had composed upon Paper which he had picked up by Accident.

Savage was characteristically indignant at being obliged to be player as well as author:

> Neither his Voice, Look nor Gesture, were such as are expected on the Stage, and he was himself so much ashamed of having been reduced to appear as a Player, that he always blotted out his Name from the List, when a Copy of his Tragedy was to be shown to his Friends.

However, the publication of the play was more successful than its performance. For this Savage was largely indebted to Aaron Hill, who also raised a subscription for his *Miscellany of Poems*. But this improvement in Savage's fortunes was quickly shattered by the quarrel in Robinson's Coffee-house, near Charing Cross, and Savage was charged with, and convicted of, the murder of James Sinclair. His pardon was subsequently granted on the plea of the Countess of Hertford. His next patron was Lord Tyrconnel who took him into his family and paid him an allowance of £200 a year. This, says Johnson, was the golden part of Savage's life:

> He was courted by all who endeavoured to be thought Men of Genius and caressed by all who valued themselves upon a refined Taste. To admire Mr *Savage* was a Proof of Discernment, and to be acquainted with him was a Title to poetical Reputation.

To this gay period belonged what Johnson regarded as Savage's masterpiece—*The Wanderer*. True, he admits that the common criticism that the poem was 'not so much a regular Fabric, as a Heap of shining materials thrown together by Accident', was probably justified; but characteristically, he insists that the poem 'can promote no other Purposes than those of Virtue and that it is written with a very strong Sense of the Efficacy of Religion'. But any period of calm or prosperity was bound to be brief. Savage was such good company in a tavern that many were prepared to pay for his wine as a cheap price for his conversational charm, but Lord Tyrconnel grew tired of his habit of bringing the tavern company home and ordering the butler to set the best wine in the cellar before them. Nor was he less indignant when he saw a collection of valuable books which he had given to Savage exposed for sale upon the stalls, 'it being usual with Mr Savage', as Johnson adds 'when he wanted a small Sum, to take his Books to the Pawnbroker'. Banished from Lord Tyrconnel's table, Savage displayed characteristic truculence. 'He returned Reproach for Reproach and Insult for Insult.' In his poem *The Bastard* he returned to the attack upon his mother's cruelty and one line, at least, has won immortality:

No tenth Transmitter of a foolish Face.

As Johnson points out, one of Savage's weaknesses lay in his imputing none of his miseries to himself. He was never made wiser by his sufferings and 'the reigning error of his life was that he mistook the Love for the Practice of Virtue...his Actions...were often blameable, but his Writings...uniformly tended to the Exaltation of the Mind and the Propagation of Morality and Piety.... These Writings may improve Mankind when his Failings shall be forgotten'. Today, Savage's works are unread and it is only his frailties that are remembered;

but for the eighteenth century Johnson's verdict held good. *Sir Thomas Overbury* was revived in 1755 with a prologue by Sheridan; his poems were reprinted in 1761 and were followed by two editions of his works.

The affair of the Laureateship was highly characteristic of Savage's fortunes and conduct. According to Johnson, he was promised the appointment by the King, but was thwarted by the Lord Chamberlain who gave the post to Colly Cibber. Savage, however, would not admit defeat. He wrote a poem with the title *Volunteer Laureat* in honour of the Queen's birthday. The verses took the Queen's fancy; and Savage was given leave to write a similar piece on future birthdays, for which he would receive an annual payment of £50:

> Great Princess! tis decreed—once ev'ry Year
> I march uncall'd your Laureat Volunteer;
> Thus shall your Poet his low Genius raise,
> And charm the World with Truths too vast for Praise.
> Nor need I dwell on Glories all your own,
> Since surer means to tempt your Smiles are known;
> Your poet shall allot your Lord his Part,
> And paint him in his noblest Throne, your Heart...

Johnson describes the Queen's desire for an annual panegyric as 'a kind of avaricious Generosity, by which Flattery was rather purchased than Genius rewarded'. The pension of £50 a year might, as Johnson says, 'have kept an exact Oeconomist from Want' but was far from being sufficient for Savage:

> No sooner had he changed the Bill, than he vanished from the Sight of all his acquaintances, and lay for some Time out of the Reach of all the Enquiries that Friendship or Curiosity could make after him.

One of his enterprises at this time was a poem addressed to the Prince of Wales entitled *On public Spirit, with regard to public Works*. Johnson quotes with special approval the lines which expose 'the enormous Wickedness of making War upon barbarous Nations because they cannot resist':

> Do you the neighb'ring, blameless *Indian* aid
> Culture what he neglects, not his invade;
> Dare not, oh! dare not, with ambitious View,
> Force or demand Subjection, never due.
> Let by *my* specious Name no *Tyrants* rise,
> And cry, while they enslave, they civilize!...
> Why must I *Afric's* sable Children see
> Vended for Slaves, though form'd by Nature free?

But the Prince took no notice of the poem or of its author and the public was similarly neglectful; only seventy-two copies were sold.

This was in 1737, the year in which Johnson first came to London, and from this date onwards Johnson was writing of what he knew:

He [Savage] lodged as much by Accident as he dined, and passed the night sometimes in mean Houses, which are set open at Night to any casual Wanderers, sometimes in Cellars... and sometimes, when he had no Money to support even the Expenses of these Receptacles, walked about the streets till he was weary....

It is in this context that we are first introduced to Savage by Boswell. Johnson, himself an adventurer in literature, was immediately attracted to Savage and especially because 'he excelled in the Arts of Conversation'. But he also realised that Savage was incorrigible:

It must therefore be acknowledged, in Justification of Mankind, that it was not always by the Negligence or Coldness of his Friends that *Savage* was distressed, but because it was in reality very difficult to preserve him long in a State of Ease. To supply him with Money was a hopeless Attempt, for no sooner did he see himself Master of a Sum sufficient to set him free from Care for a Day, than he became profuse and luxurious.

In 1738 the death of the Queen and the coldness of the Prince deprived Savage of his pension, and his friends, headed by Pope, raised a subscription to provide him with a similar allowance on condition that he should retire from London and live quietly at Swansea. Savage accepted the condition and, as Johnson says, 'planned out a Scheme of Life for the Country'. Johnson, as always, was profoundly scornful of any prospect of rural enjoyment.

Savage [he writes] was gently reproached by a Friend [no doubt Johnson himself] for submitting to live upon a Subscription but 'he could not bear to debar himself from the Happiness which was to be found in the Calm of a Cottage or lose the Opportunity of listening, without intermission, to the Melody of the Nightingale which he believed was to be heard from every Bramble and which he did not fail to mention as a very important Part of the Happiness of a Country Life'.

Years later this scorn of pastoral bliss was developed in *Idler*, no. 71. Savage left London in 1739, parting from Johnson with tears in his eyes and a promise of 'strict Adherence to his Maxims of Parsimony'. A fortnight later news came that he was still on the road and that his money was exhausted. Eventually he reached Swansea, completed the revision of his tragedy and said he must return to London to produce it. His friends very naturally protested against this and reduced the allowance paid to Savage. Furious, he made his way to Bristol, was hospitably received by a number of friends and straightway abused their hospitality. When money arrived from London, it was promptly spent, not on the discharge of his debts but at his favourite tavern. Gravitation to a debtor's prison was inevitable and it was there on 1 August 1743 that he died.

In his summing-up Johnson is torn between the sympathy of a friend and the obligation of a moralist. Savage, he says, was 'equally distinguished by his Virtues and Vices and at once remarkable for his Weaknesses and Abilities'. His temper was capricious, his friendship was of little value and he thought himself born to be supported by others. On the other hand, he knew how to practise all the graces of conversation and if he outstayed his welcome, it was frequently because he might have to spend the rest of the night in the street. Johnson would allow no judgment based on Pharisaical superiority; but his final sentence embodies the ultimate warning of the moralist: 'Negligence and Irregularity, long continued, will make knowledge useless, Wit ridiculous and Genius contemptible.'

This brief survey is designed not primarily as a picture of the extraordinary career of Richard Savage, but as an illustration of Johnson's biographical method. Perhaps 'method' is the wrong word. The *Life* of Savage was written at a great pace and at white heat; for orderly research Johnson had neither the time nor the inclination. Apart from short lives of Thomas Browne and Roger Ascham, written as introductions to their works, he did not return to biography until he was commissioned many years later to write similar introductions to the collection of the English poets. In so far as he enjoyed any kind of writing, he enjoyed the compilation of these lives. If a particular poet's writing raised fundamental questions of literary criticism, he would supplement the life with an expanded critical essay, as he did, for example, in his treatment of Cowley or Pope; if a particular work made no appeal to him, he said so: on Thomson's *Liberty*, he wrote: 'When it first appeared, I tried to read, and soon desisted. I have never tried again, and therefore will not hazard either praise or censure.'

When he came to include the *Life* of Savage in the collection it was characteristic of him that he hazarded neither revision nor expansion.

4. *DR JOHNSON AND THE FAIRIES*[1]

'BEFORE they go out into school life,' wrote Andrew Lang, 'many little fellows of nine, or so, are extremely original, imaginative and almost poetical.... I have known a little boy who liked to lie on the grass and to people the alleys and glades of that miniature forest with fairies and dwarfs, whom he seemed actually to see in a kind of vision. But he went to school; he instantly won the hundred yards race for boys under twelve and he came back a young barbarian, interested in "the theory of touch" (at football), curious in the art of bowling and no more capable than you and I of seeing fairies in a green meadow'.

In one of his best known essays ('Rupert Brooke and the Intellectual Imagination'), Walter de la Mare records a similar series of observations and contemplates them in relation to the making of poetry. Imagination,

[1] Printed in *Tribute to Walter de la Mare* (1948).

he says, the imagination that not merely invents, but that creates, is an essential quality of the poet and is of two distinct types: 'The one divines, the other discovers. The one is intuitive, inductive; the other logical, deductive. The one visionary, the other intellectual. The one knows that beauty is truth, the other proves that truth is beauty. And the poet inherits, as it seems to me, the one kind from the child in him, the other from the boy in him.'

And what is the peg on which this distinction is hung? A sonnet of Keats? An outburst by Blake? A stanza from *The Ancient Mariner*? No, it hangs upon a remark of Dr Johnson's.

On an evening in 1766, Goldsmith and Boswell had been asking Johnson why he had given up going to the play and writing verses. 'Why, Sir,' was the reply, 'our tastes greatly alter. The lad does not care for the child's rattle...' and, omitting Johnson's slightly Rabelaisian amplification of the argument, de la Mare builds his theory of the two sorts of poetical imagination upon the changing tastes of the lad who outgrows childish things.

How deep would have been Johnson's astonishment if he had been able to follow the germination of the seed he had casually sown. True, he had declared through the mouth of Imlac that nothing could be useless to a poet; that whatever was beautiful or dreadful, or awfully vast or elegantly little must be familiar to his imagination. But what did Johnson mean by 'imagination'? In his *Dictionary* he distinguished two main senses: first, that of the act of imagining: 'Fancy; the power of forming ideal pictures; the power of representing things absent to one's self or others', and second, that of the thing imagined: 'Conception; image in the mind; idea', and it is characteristic that one of his quotations is from *Samson Agonistes*:

> O whither shall I run, or which way fly
> The sight of this so horrid spectacle,
> Which erst my eyes beheld, and yet behold!
> For dire imagination still pursues me.

It was the dangers, rather than the delights, of the imaginative faculty that impressed themselves upon Johnson's mind. In the 89th number of *The Rambler* he had proclaimed a solemn warning to those who gave themselves up to the luxury of fancy:

There is nothing more fatal to a man whose business it is to think than to have learned the art of regaling his mind with those airy gratifications. Other vices or follies are restrained by fear, reformed by admonition, or rejected by the conviction which the comparison of our conduct with that of others may in time produce. But this invisible riot of the mind, this secret prodigality of being is secure from detection and fearless of reproach. The dreamer retires to his apartments, shuts out the cares and interruptions of mankind, and abandons himself to his own fancy; new worlds rise up before him, one image is followed by another, and a long succession of delights dances round him. He is at last called back to life by nature, or by custom, and enters peevish into society, because he cannot model it to his own will. He returns from his idle excursions with the asperity, though not with the knowledge of a student, and hastens again to the same felicity with the eagerness of a man bent upon the advancement of some favourite science. The infatuation strengthens by degrees, and, like the poison of opiates, weakens his powers, without any external symptom of malignity.

This, it may well be said, is the moralist's censure of idleness rather than the critic's estimate of the value of poetic imagination, and in the 44th chapter of *Rasselas*, with its solemn title, 'The Dangerous Prevalence of Imagination', the same warning is delivered by Imlac:

> To indulge the power of fiction, and send imagination out upon the wing, is often the sport of those who delight too much in silent speculation. When we are alone we are not always busy; the labour of excogitation is too violent to last long; the ardour of inquiry will sometimes give way to idleness or satiety. He who has nothing external that can divert him must find pleasure in his own thoughts, and must conceive himself what he is not; for who is pleased with what he is? He then expatiates in boundless futurity and culls from all imaginable conditions that which for the present moment he should most desire, amuses his desires with impossible enjoyments and confers upon his pride unattainable dominion.

'For who is pleased with what he is?' That, in effect, was the theme of Johnson's own *Prayers and Meditations*, that pathetic and revealing record of candid self-appraisal, of recurrent despair, and of undaunted resolution. Commentators[1] have analysed in detail Johnson's distrust of the imagination and the intensity of the forces that strove for the mastery in his mind. It was a constant struggle and in his familiar letters, as well as in his formal essays, Johnson continually dwelt upon the dangers of solitude and of the foolish imaginings which it inevitably fostered. Thus he wrote to Elizabeth Aston: 'Some communication of sentiments is commonly necessary to give vent to the imagination and discharge the mind of its own flatulencies', and to Mrs Thrale: 'The use of travelling is to regulate imagination by reality and instead of thinking

[1] E.g. W. B. C. Watkins, *Perilous Balance* (Princeton, 1939); R. D. Havens, *Johnson's Distrust of the Imagination* (E. L. H., 1943); and B. H. Bronson, *Johnson Agonistes* (Cambridge, 1946).

DR JOHNSON AND THE FAIRIES

how things may be, to see them as they are.' There were, in Johnson's view, two ways in which the human mind could be employed: it could, on the one hand, be engaged in argument or in instruction or in the negotiation of business or in various other activities involving association with other human beings; or, on the other hand, it could be engaged in study and creative work in solitude. So long as a man was absorbed in an occupation which brought him into touch with other men, his mental stability and his practical usefulness were assured; but once he withdrew himself to solitude, he was at the mercy of 'an invisible riot of the mind'. To Johnson, indeed, 'imagination' suggested little of the lovely solemnity of a child's make-believe and nothing of the delights of a poet's day-dreaming. He was, of course, endowed with a large measure of imaginative sympathy—so large, indeed, that he was frightened by it. His sensitiveness to Shakespearian tragedy is well known. The deaths of Cordelia and of Desdemona were almost more than he could endure. So, when he talked of putting aside playgoing and verse-writing as a child puts aside his rattle, perhaps he reflected that other, less disturbing, kinds of literary activity suited him better—lexicography had been safe and critical biography was congenial. The powers of imagination as conceived, for instance, by Akenside (those powers which 'hold a middle place between the organs of bodily sense and the faculties of moral perception'), held no terrors for him and he appraised *The Pleasures of the Imagination* with a light heart:

His images are displayed with such luxuriance of expression that...the reader wanders through the gay diffusion, sometimes amazed and sometimes delighted; but after many turnings in the flowery labyrinth, comes out as he went in. He remarked little and laid hold on nothing.

Akenside's profusion of imagery was as harmless in Johnson's eyes as Shenstone's 'ambition for rural elegance'.

But neither rural elegance nor rural simplicity offered any consolation to Johnson. When de la Mare contemplates the time when dust must surrender to dust, he prays:

> May the rusting harvest hedgerow
> Still the Traveller's Joy entwine
> And as happy children gather
> Posies once mine.

Hedgerows and posies had no place in Johnson's meditations upon death. The thought of annihilation was terrible to him and when he could bear to talk of the subject more lightly, his reflections were incorrigibly urban: 'An odd thought strikes me—we shall receive no letters in the grave.' When he came to the criticism of *A Midsummer Night's Dream* he noted with pleasure 'Our Author's admirable description of the miseries of the Country' and his comment upon Shakespeare's fairyland is significant: 'Fairies in his time were much in fashion.'

Yet, even in Johnson's time, they had not gone wholly out of fashion, and it is not to be forgotten that Johnson himself was the author of a fairy-tale. Just about the time of his discussion with Goldsmith and Boswell about the writing of verses, he had contributed to the *Miscellanies* of Anna Williams a tale entitled 'The Fountains'. It was the story of Floretta, a kind-hearted little girl who at the foot of Plinlimmon saw a lovely goldfinch entangled by a lime-twig with a hawk hovering over him. Floretta had the courage to defy the hawk and to rescue the goldfinch and refused to let her mother imprison him in a cage. Whereupon the bird turned out to be the chief of the fairies in disguise and Floretta was given as reward the power of indulging any wish that she might have and also the liberty of retracting it. Beauty, wealth, wit, length of life were the successive objects of her petitions and each brought disillusion and misery. It is Johnson's perpetual theme—the vanity of human wishes. But Johnson did his best to adapt himself to fairyland and braced himself to a description of his fairy queen:

> When she [Floretta] entered the thicket, and was near the place for which she was looking, from behind a blossoming hawthorn advanced a female form of very low stature, but of elegant proportion and majestick air, arrayed in all the colours of the meadow, and sparkling as she moved like a dew-drop in the sun.

How would Floretta have been depicted and how would her story have been told by someone capable of seeing fairies in a green meadow? Perhaps Walter de la Mare could have told us. For had he, too, not stood behind a hawthorn bush and

> Watched on the fairies flaxen-tressed
> The fires of the morning flush?

IV. THOMAS GRAY OF PEMBROKE[1]

To Victorian readers the most familiar estimate of Thomas Gray was that presented by Matthew Arnold in the famous essay in which he described Gray as a poet born into a prosaic age and matriculated into an uninspired and uninspiring university. In particular, Arnold made extravagant play with a simple remark made in describing Gray's reticence about his last illness—'He never spoke out.'

'In these four words', says Arnold, 'is contained the whole history of Gray as a man and a poet.' Here is oversimplification *in excelsis*, but Arnold could use a phrase of this kind with extraordinary skill, and it was left to later commentators to demolish the elaborate structure built on so slender a foundation. A recent essay by a distinguished predecessor of mine in this lectureship, Lord David Cecil, contains a much more sensitive and more penetrating analysis of Gray's poetic temperament. But even here there is, perhaps, undue emphasis laid upon Gray's solitariness in the society of eighteenth-century dons—'stodgy celibates', in Lord David's view, 'who, having risen from narrow circumstances, had relaxed for the rest of their lives into a monotonous existence of over-eating, over-drinking and petty college business'.

Here and there in this unpromising milieu Lord David admits that a scholar occasionally appeared; he admits,

[1] W. P. Ker Memorial Lecture, Glasgow, 1952.

too, that Gray formed a number of friendships and that he derived some amusement from the life that went on around him. But it was a detached amusement—'As from a box in a theatre,' writes Lord David, 'he sat gazing from the window of his rooms at the comedy of University life. But he did not go down on to the stage.' On this it may be sufficient, for the moment, to observe that what is presented on the stage is but the final product of theatrical effort. What of the whispering in the wings and the gossip in the green room? What of the varied and ceaseless activity behind the scenes? Behind the scenes—and especially the Pembroke scenes—of the drama of eighteenth-century Cambridge, there was to be found the figure of Thomas Gray, shy and solitary by temperament, but frequently moved to lively interest and activity and certainly much more than an amused spectator.

Gray's first introduction to the Cambridge scene was in the Michaelmas Term of 1734, when he came up to Peterhouse as a freshman from Eton. From the first he looked upon Cambridge with a satirical eye:

I warrant, you imagine, [he wrote to Walpole on 31 October] that people in one College, know the Customs of others; but you mistake, they are quite little Societies by themselves: ye Dresses, Language, Customs &c are quite different in different Colledges: what passes for Wit in one, would not be understood if it were carried to another: thus the Men of Peter-house, Pembroke and Clare-Hall of course must be Tories; those of Trinity, Rakes; of Kings, Scholars; of Sidney, Wigs; of St. Johns, Worthy men and so on...there are 5 ranks in the University, subordinate to the Vice-chancellour, who is chose annually: these are Masters, Fellows, Fellow-Commoners, Pensioners and Sizers; the Masters of Colledges are twelve grey-hair'd Gentlefolks, who are all mad with Pride; the Fellows are sleepy, drunken, dull, illiterate Things; the Fellow-Com: are imitatours of the Fellows, or else Beaux, or else nothing: the Pension: grave formal Sots, who would be thought old; or else drink Ale and sing Songs against ye Excise. The Sizers are Graziers Eldest Sons, who come to get good Learning, that they may all be Archbishops of Canterbury: these 2 last Orders are qualified to take Scholarships; one of which, your humble Servt has had given him...

Such were the impressions of a freshman of three weeks' standing. No doubt, a certain measure of observation lay behind them, but they owed more to the exuberance of Gray's epistolary fancy. They are an early and vivid illustration of Walpole's remark that 'Gray never wrote anything easily but things of humour; humour was his natural and original turn'.

At the beginning of his second term he wrote in a similarly ironic vein about his studies:

I have made such a wonderful progress in Philosophy, that I begin to be quite persuaded, that black is white and that fire will not burn, and that I ought not, either to give credit to my eyes or feeling; they tell me too, that I am nothing in the world, and that I only fancy, I exist....

More congenial than the routine of metaphysics and mathematics were private lessons in Italian and the exchange of poetic translation and criticism with his schoolfellow, West; and early in his third year Gray obtained leave not to proceed to a degree:

After this term [he wrote to West in December 1736] I shall have nothing more of college impertinencies to undergo ...I have endured lectures daily and hourly since I came last.

But, characteristically, he did not wish to desert the study of philosophy, provided that he was a free agent:

Here I am [he wrote to Walpole] a little happy to think, I shan't take Degree's; and really, now I know there is no occasion, I don't know but I may read a little Philosophy; it is sufficient to make a thing agreeable, not to have much need of it: such is my humour....

Amongst the lectures which Gray appears to have endured were those of one with whom he was destined to be long associated. This was Roger Long, D.D., Master of Pembroke from 1733 to 1770 and first Lowndean Professor of Astronomy and Geometry, who was at this time lecturing on experimental philosophy.

My motions... [wrote Gray to Walpole] are much like those of a Pendulum, or (Dr Longically speaking) oscillatory, I swing from Chapell or Hall home, and from home to chapell or hall.

It is clear that even as an undergraduate Gray was not wholly detached from the University, and certainly he made more than one friend in Pembroke. Having some reputation as a Latin versifier, he contributed in 1736 to the Cambridge volume of congratulations on the Marriage of the Prince of Wales and in the same year one of the Moderators for the Tripos asked him to write the Tripos verses for distribution, in accordance with custom, with the list of successful candidates. Gray's subject was *Luna Habitabilis* and the Moderator was James Brown, Fellow of Pembroke, who was to be one of the most faithful friends of Gray's whole life. Another early friendship was that with Thomas Wharton, who came up to Pembroke at the same time that Gray was admitted to Peterhouse and afterwards became a fellow. 'My dear dear Wharton', wrote Gray in 1740, '(which is a dear more than I give any body else).'

Gray remained at Peterhouse until September 1738. Of Cambridge he continued to write with undergraduate scorn, yet he found it hard to leave:

> I don't know how it is, I have a sort of reluctance to leave this place, unamiable as it may seem; 'tis true Cambridge is very ugly, she is very dirty and very dull; but I'm like a cabbage, where I'm stuck, I love to grow....

and later:

> I am at this instant in the very agonies of leaving college, and would not wish the worst of my enemies a worse situation. If you knew the dust, the old boxes, the bedsteads and tutors that are about my ears, you would look upon this letter as a great effort of my resolution and unconcernedness in the midst of evils.

Gray had been admitted to the Inner Temple in 1735 and had planned to join his friend West there on going down from Cambridge. But when Walpole invited him to make an extended tour in France and Italy, he very naturally changed his plans. The travellers embarked at Dover in the spring of 1739 and Gray did not return to England until the summer of 1741. Some of Gray's letters descriptive of the grandeur of mountain scenery have become famous in the history of travel and in the history of the romantic movement and on his second visit to the Grande Chartreuse he was moved to write a Latin ode in which he prayed for gentle quietude in his youth (*placidam juveni quietem*) and for a secluded corner in which to pass his later years:

> *Saltem remoto des, Pater, angulo*
> *Horas senectae ducere liberas;*
> *Tutumque vulgari tumultu*
> *Surripias, hominumque curis.*

Here the 'madding crowd' and the 'sequestr'd vale' appear in their original Latinity. The end of Gray's sojourn abroad was marred by a serious quarrel with his friend and benefactor, Horace Walpole. The exact circumstances of the quarrel have never been fully revealed; probably the benefactor in Walpole predominated too often over the friend.

Gray now clung to West as the principal pleasure he had to hope for in his own country. To West he analysed his feelings about poetry, about society and about himself.

You must add then, to your former idea, [he wrote from Florence in April 1741] two years of age, reasonable quantity of dullness, a great deal of silence, and something that rather resembles, than is, thinking; a confused notion of many strange and fine things that have swum before my eyes for some time, a want of love for general society, indeed an inability to it. On the good side you may add a sensibility for what others feel, and indulgence for their faults or weaknesses, a love of truth, and detestation of everything else. Then you are to deduct a little impertinence, a little laughter, a great deal of pride, and some spirits....

There follows a farewell to Florence in Latin hexameters and, after Gray's return to England in September, there was a continuous exchange of poetry, poetic criticism, and poetic translation. Early in June 1742 Gray wrote to West from Stoke Poges. The letter was returned to him unopened, for West was dead. Gray first heard the news from some verses published in a newspaper a fortnight later and was overwhelmed by grief and loneliness. With his last letter to West he had enclosed his *Ode on the Spring* and in August he wrote a sonnet to the memory of his friend:

> The Fields to all their wonted Tribute bear:
> To warm their little Loves the Birds complain:
> I fruitless mourn to him, that cannot hear,
> And weep the more because I weep in vain.

In the same month he wrote, though he did not publish, his *Ode on a Distant Prospect of Eton College* and the *Hymn to Adversity*.

Death had robbed Gray of one of his best friends and a quarrel had separated him from another. His father had died and his mother's poor circumstances made it necessary for him to determine how his life should be spent. One possibility was that of practising law in London. But this was not a congenial prospect and Gray decided to return to Cambridge and read Law there. By the Michaelmas Term he was in residence again at Peterhouse as a fellow-commoner and up to a point took his legal studies seriously. With his Pembroke friends he quickly renewed contact. William Trollope, at that time a Fellow, arranged for him to borrow books from the Pembroke library and Gray wrote to Wharton in December 1743:

> Mr Trollope, I suppose, has told you how I was employed a part of the Time; how by my own indefatigable Application for these ten Years past... I am got half way to the Top of Jurisprudence....'

by which he meant that he had qualified for the degree of LL.B. Cambridge, he goes on to tell Wharton, is as it was and the People as they were. But characteristically he hints at a scandal about the Vice-Chancellor, and adds in a postscript:

> Won't you come to the Jubilee? Dr Long is to dance a Saraband and Hornpipe of his own Invention without lifting either Foot once from the Ground.

The reference is to the celebration on New Year's Day 1743 of the 400th anniversary of the foundation of Pembroke College. Gray's allusion to the Master, Roger Long, is, as usual, satirical. In 1743 Long had been Master for ten years. He had been elected Fellow of the Royal Society in 1729 and the first volume of his work on astronomy had been published in 1742. He had a passion for musical and mechanical invention: he built a hollow sphere with a revolving roof showing the movements of the heavenly bodies, a scholar being paid to work the crank for the benefit of visitors; in his garden he contrived a 'water work' in the form of 'a beautiful and large Bason ... wherein he often diverts himself in a Machine of his own contrivance, to go with the foot as he rides therein'; on the ground floor of his Lodge he had a printing-press on which some of his astronomical works were produced; and the Lodge, as a whole, was stocked with mathematical and musical instruments. As an author, he did not restrict himself to scientific subjects; he wrote pamphlets on Church Defence and on Greek Accents and also a *Life* of Mahomet. At the age of eighty he had an audience of the King and Queen to whom he presented a lyricord of his own invention; he had become Vice-Chancellor immediately after his election as Master and at the age of eighty-nine he was nominated for a second tenure of the office. But even unreformed Cambridge felt that some risk might be involved and he was not elected. In all his scientific activities Long had a remarkable helper in the person of Richard Dunthorne. Long took him from a country grammar school into his household service; there he continued to pursue his studies and for a time became a schoolmaster, but Long quickly recalled him to Pembroke and for many years he combined in a remarkable way the duties of College Butler and scientific assistant to the Master. Few men have left records of competence in such diverse employments. On the one hand there are his astronomical works including *The Practical Astronomy of the Moon*, published at the University Press in 1739, and many communications to the Royal Society; on the other, there are the Pembroke Buttery Books, all written in his beautiful hand and showing those in residence week by week and day by day until his retirement in 1771, when he was succeeded by Gray's servant, Stephen Hempstead.

Dunthorne was no doubt intimately concerned with the celebrations of 1743, but little documentary detail has survived save the Secular Ode composed for the occasion by Christopher Smart. Smart was at that time a Bachelor Scholar of the College and celebrated the glories of the College with great gusto: the Foundress and past members of the College are duly invoked; in particular Edmund Spenser, 'peerless bard', as Smart calls him, though he gives him an erroneous Christian name. The Ode concludes:

> Religious joy, and sober pleasure,
> Virtuous ease, and learned leisure,
> Society and books, that give
> Th' important lesson how to live:
> These are gifts, are gifts divine,
> For, fair Pembroke, these were thine.

The occasion, no doubt, was a convivial one and Gray's reference to it suggests that he may have been present as the guest of Trollope or Brown. It is, perhaps, characteristic of the casual antiquarianism of the period that the jubilee was held four years too soon. The College was founded in 1347.

Gray's interest in Pembroke affairs persisted. A friend of his, Henry Tuthill, who had graduated from Peterhouse in 1743 and had been ordained in the following year, migrated to Pembroke in 1746. In October of that year he was duly nominated for election to a Fellowship and received seven votes as against four given for another candidate, Thomas Knowles. The voting is clearly recorded in the College Register, but at the foot there is written in the Master's hand: *Ego non consentio. R. Long.* This action induced a major crisis. Had the Master a right to this veto? Legal opinion seemed to suggest that he had. The College statutes at that time contained no provision for a Visitor and further controversy arose as to whether the proper arbitrator were the King or the Chancellor of the University. Deadlock followed and there was bitter enmity between Roger Long and the Fellows.

Mr Brown [wrote Gray to Wharton in December 1746] (who I assure you holds up his Head and his Spirits very notably) will give you an Account of your College Proceedings, if they may be so call'd, where nothing proceeds at all. Only the last Week Roger was so wise to declare *ex motu proprio* that he took Mr Delaval (who is now a Fell: Commoner) into his own Tuition...they all came to an Eclaircissement in the Parlour, they abused him pretty reasonably, and it ended in threatening them as usual with a Visitor. in short they are all as rude as may be, leave him at Table by himself, never go into the Parlour, till he comes out; or if he enters when they are there, continue sitting even in his own Magesterial Chair. May bickers with him publickly about twenty paltry Matters and Roger t'other Day told him he was impertinent. What would you have more?....

Roger Long's patronage of John Blake Delaval was unfortunate. The young man was found to be showing the sights of Cambridge to a certain Nell Burnet disguised in an officer's uniform and bearing the *nom de guerre* of Captain Hargreaves.

> The Master [Gray wrote to Wharton] raised his Posse-Comitatus in Order to search his Chambers and after long Feeling and Snuffleing about the Bed, he declared they had certainly been there. wch was very true....

So Mr Delaval went down from College. It is consoling to note that he was afterwards raised to the peerage and was buried in Westminster Abbey.

Meanwhile the major controversy dragged on. In November 1747 another friend of Gray's, William Mason of St John's, was duly nominated for election to a Fellowship at Pembroke. Again the Master applied his veto and submitted a formal appeal to the Chancellor of the University; the Chancellor prudently referred the question to the Vice-Chancellor. But the Fellows were also active and obtained a Writ of Prohibition from the Court of King's Bench. For once, Long recognised that he was beaten; his one consolation was that his own candidate, Knowles, was elected Fellow together with Tuthill and Mason.

Gray made a point of recording the details for Wharton's benefit:

> So Roger, believing them unanimous (after some few Pribbles and Prabbles) said, well then, if it be for ye Good of ye College—but you intend Knowles shall be Senior—To be sure, Master—Well then, and so they proceeded to Election and all was over in a few Minutes.

In 1745, Christopher Smart had been elected to a Fellowship without controversy. Amongst other activities he wrote a comedy entitled *A Trip to Cambridge or the Grateful Fair* which was performed in the Hall of Pembroke in 1747. 'He acts five parts himself,' wrote Gray, 'and is only sorry, he can't do all the rest.' Smart's Cambridge career was erratic. Brown and two other Fellows of the College came to his rescue when he was threatened with imprisonment for debt and Gray, though rightly foreseeing that he would end in jail or bedlam, pleaded charitably to Wharton: 'Yet one would try to save him, for Drunkenness is one great source of all this and he may change it.' The establishment of the Seatonian Prize for a poem on the Perfections or Attributes of the Supreme Being gave Smart an opportunity which he was quick to seize. He went out of residence in 1749, but he won the prize for five years out of six between 1750 and 1755.

Unfortunately, he broke other rules besides those of sobriety. On 27 November 1753 the College ordered 'that the dividend assign'd to Mr Smart be deposited in the treasury till the society be satisfied that he has a right to the same; it being credibly reported that he has been married for some time'.

The report was true; but Smart was allowed 'to keep his name in the College books, without any expence, so long as he continues to write for the premium left by Mr Seaton'.

Meanwhile, Gray had succumbed to the spirit of Cambridge; it was, he said the spirit of Lazyness:

Time will settle my Conscience, Time will reconcile me to this languid Companion: we shall smoke, we shall tipple, we shall doze together. We shall have our little Jokes, like other People and our long Stories; Brandy will finish what Port begun....

and then he proceeds to forecast the inaccurate notice of his death that would appear in the *London Evening Post*. Willy-nilly, Cambridge was claiming him for her own. Pembroke, he tells Wharton, is all harmonious and delightful since the pacification, but badly in need of freshmen.

In July 1749 the Duke of Newcastle was installed as Chancellor of the University, the Master of Magdalene (Thomas Chapman) being Vice-Chancellor. For both of these dignitaries Gray had a profound contempt and wrote with scorn of the Vice-Chancellor's eloquence. 'Vesuvio in an Eruption', he said, 'was not more violent than his Utterance.' During the celebrations, he told Wharton, everyone was very gay and very busy in the Morning and very owlish and very tipsy at Night. The only item that pleased Gray was the ode written by his friend Mason and set to music by Mr Boyce, Composer to His Majesty. Mason was rapidly growing into Gray's good graces and, in particular, seemed likely to help Brown and Tuthill in improving the status of Pembroke. Gray was also anxious to secure a Fellowship for his Peterhouse friend, Stonehewer, but hesitated to make an attempt on Pembroke, in view of the danger of the Master 'playing his old game'. Wharton was by this time medically qualified and was contemplating the possibility of practising either in Bath or Cambridge. Gray was not encouraging about Cambridge:

You are aware undoubtedly that a certain Deference, not to say Servility, to the Heads of Colleges, is perhaps necessary to a Physician, that means to establish himself here: you possibly may find a Method to do without it. another Inconvenience your Wife, rather than you, will feel, the Want of Company of her own sex; as the Women are few here, squeezy and formal, and little skill'd in amusing themselves or other People.

At the same time (October 1751) he was able to tell Wharton that Pembroke was picking up; there were twelve freshmen and two new Fellows, including Edward Hussey Delaval, brother of the unfortunate J. B. Delaval and later a distinguished man of science. His famous set of musical glasses was to give Gray great pleasure in later years. Later, in 1755, the Pembroke high table was graced by the admission of the ninth Earl of Strathmore as a fellow-commoner and two of his brothers followed shortly afterwards.

It would, of course, be wrong to suggest that, at this or any other period, Gray was wholly absorbed in university and college affairs. Between 1742, when he returned to Cambridge, and 1755 the *Eton Ode*, the *Elegy* and the *Six Poems with Bentley's Designs* had been published and the *Bard* and the *Ode on Vicissitude* begun; a reconciliation with Walpole had been effected and with him, as with others, Gray had much correspondence on literary and antiquarian topics. But it is clear that his intense interest in the conduct of affairs in Pembroke and his devotion to his Pembroke friends were prominent in his day-to-day life and thought—and all this before he had become a member of the College.

Early in 1756 occurred the famous incident of the fire-alarm at Peterhouse. Apart from embroideries uncritically accepted by some later biographers, certain facts are known. Gray's rooms were on the second floor of the northern wing of Peterhouse. Having a dread of fire he asked Walpole to procure a rope-ladder and the bar he affixed outside his window from which it was to be suspended is still there for every tourist to see. A reliable contemporary account states that some rowdy members of Peterhouse, led by Lord Percival, a fellow-commoner of Magdalene, thought it would be no bad diversion, as they said, to make Gray bolt and so ordered their man to roar out 'Fire!' Gray appeared at the window in a white night-cap and then, realising the hoax, went back to bed. But he was exceedingly angry. It was not the first time he had been annoyed by Peterhouse rowdies and he laid a formal complaint before the Master, Dr Law. The Master dismissed the incident as a boyish frolic and Gray took immediate action. He moved across the road and the Pembroke Admission Book contains the following entry under 6 March 1756: 'Thomas Gray, LL.B. admissus est ex Collegio Divi Petri.' On 25 March Gray wrote:

> This may be look'd upon as a sort of Aera in a life so barren of events as mine.... I am for the present extremely well lodged here, and as quiet as in the Grande Chartreuse...everybody (even the Dr Longs and Dr Mays) are as civil as they could be to Mary de Valence in person.

In the summer he went to Stoke Poges and, while he was there, learnt that Roger Long, then aged seventy-six, was either dying or dead. Immediately he busied himself to secure votes for James Brown as Long's successor in the Mastership. He urged Walpole to say a word to the Duke of Bedford and warned him against a possible rival in Leonard Addison, one of the senior Fellows of the College. At the same time he sent a similar warning to Mason: Addison, a good Whig, would be likely to get the support of many influential people and Gray suggests that, if Mason would stand, he might split the vote and then withdraw and let Brown in.

If you can divide or carry this interest and by it gain the dirty part of the College, so as to throw it into Mr B.'s scale at pleasure, perhaps it may produce an unanimous election. This struck me last night as a practicable thing. But I see some danger in it, for you may disoblige your own friends....

Having thus carried us forward to the atmosphere of Mark Pattison's *Memoirs*, or indeed to that of Mr Snow's recent novel *The Masters*, Gray proceeds to analyse the list of fellows and to mark those who might reasonably be expected to vote for Brown. But at the end of the letter he shrewdly adds: 'Dr L:, if he is not dead, will recover. Mind, if he don't.' Gray was right. Roger Long lived for another fourteen years.

The Society into which Gray had been admitted as a fellow-commoner was a small one. At the high table were the Master, James Brown the President (or Vice-Master), twelve Fellows and six Fellow-commoners including the Earl of Strathmore and his brother, James Philip Lyon; at the lower table were twenty-three Bachelors and undergraduates. Of the Fellows two-thirds were in holy orders and every year an impressive series of college appointments was made—Treasurer, Bursar, Dean, Chaplain, Catechist as well as Praelectors in Philosophy, Greek, Hebrew and Literae Humaniores. The Fellows may not have been markedly industrious but, as a body, they were far from being stagnant. A few settled down to conduct the affairs of the College, but the majority moved on after a few years to country livings and matrimonial freedom. In the words of the motto which Gray ascribed to Dr Plumptre, President of Queens', '*Non magna loquimur, sed vivimus*, i.e. We don't say much but we hold good livings'.

In fact, the personnel of an eighteenth-century high table changed much more rapidly than in later times and whatever may have been the shortcomings of the Fellows, senility was not one of them. When Gray moved across the road to Pembroke, his friend and sponsor, James Brown, was forty-seven; the average age of the rest of the Fellows was thirty.

With long-standing friendships behind him, Gray was quickly at home in his new College. When he was asked by Lord John Cavendish to recommend a private tutor for his nephew, a prospective freshman, Gray did his best to be impartial, but his desire, he said, was to bring him to Pembroke. One of his protégés, however, Henry Tuthill, was a source of bitter, and even tragic disappointment. Less than a year after Gray's migration the following entries appear in the College Register:

Feb. 2 1757

This day the Master, in the presence of 5 fellows declared Mr Tuthill's Fellowship to be vacant, he having been absent from the College above a month contrary to the Statutes, which inflicts that punishment upon such absence.

Since Mr Tuthill's absence, common fame has laid him under violent suspicion of having been guilty of great enormities; to clear himself from which he has not made his appearance and there is good reason to believe he never will.

The nature of these enormities has never been revealed.

Later in 1757, Gray was busy with the proofs of his odes on the *Progress of Poesy* and the *Bard*, which were printed at Horace Walpole's press at Strawberry Hill, and he was careful to send copies to the Master and resident Fellows of Pembroke as well as to the Master of St John's, the Master of Corpus and other dons. He had a keen eye for typographical minutiae:

> Dodsley sent me some copies last week [he wrote to Walpole] they are very pleasant to the eye and will do no dishonour to your Press. As you are but young in the trade, you will excuse me if I tell you, that some little inaccuracies have escaped your eye....

And he goes on to complain of misplacings of apostrophes and commas, vividly recalling to my recollection similar, but more vitriolic, protests made by another lonely poet who became a Cambridge don, the late A. E. Housman.

As to the poems themselves, Gray had deliberately labelled them φωνᾶντα συνετοῖσι, but the συνετοί, he said, were even fewer than he expected:

> All people of condition are agreed not to admire, nor even to understand: one very great man, writing to an acquaintance of his and mine, says that he had read them seven or eight times, and that now, when he next sees him, he shall not have above thirty questions to ask.... Even my friends tell me they do not succeed, and write me moving topics of consolation on that head; in short, I have heard of nobody but a player and a doctor of divinity that profess their esteem for them....

The player was David Garrick and the doctor of divinity 'Estimate' Brown. But Gray had a perfectly clear notion of poetic fame. He refused the Laureateship when it was offered to him and had 'no relish for any other fame than what is conferred by the few real Judges, that are so thinly scatter'd over the face of the earth'.

It is one of the ironies of literary history that this should have been written by the author of the *Elegy*, the poem that provoked Johnson's famous dictum that the common reader was the final arbiter of poetical honours.

In 1760 Gray, like many middle-aged dons of all periods, was beginning to appreciate Cambridge for its own sake:

> Cambridge is a delight of a place, now there is nobody in it. I do believe you would like it if you knew what it was like without inhabitants. It is they, I assure you, that get it an ill name and spoil all. Our friend Dr Chapman (one of its nuisances) is not expected here again in a hurry. He is gone to his grave with five fine mackerel (large and full of roe) in his belly. He eat them all at one dinner; but his fate was a turbot on Trinity Sunday, of which he left little for the company besides bones. He had not been hearty all the week; but after this sixth fish he never held up his head more.... They say he made a very good end.

Poor Dr Chapman! Dead or alive he was frequently the object of Gray's epistolary scorn. Years before he had written contemptuously of his sycophancy at the time of the Duke of Newcastle's installation as Chancellor and now he repeated the story of his death to three separate correspondents.

But even in Gray's view not all Cambridge inhabitants were nuisances. In November 1761 he urges Mason to 'come to Cambridge out of hand, for here is Mr Dillival and a charming set of Glasses, that sing like nightingales, and we have concerts every other night and shall stay here this month or two, and a vast deal of good company'.

Like all good letter-writers, Gray charms by his inconsistency. At one time he may describe Cambridge as a place where no events grow; at another as 'fruitful enough of events to furnish out many paragraphs'. But whatever the introduction, the hotch-potch of gossip follows—an unexpected visit from Walpole, Roger Long's audience at Buckingham House, the importance and absurdities of Rousseau's *Emile*, the prospect of a change of government, nature notes made in the garden of Pembroke.

In the autumn of 1765 Gray made an excursion to the Highlands and stayed with the Earl of Strathmore at Glamis Castle, of which he wrote a detailed description to Wharton. While he was there, he made the acquaintance of James Beattie and through him received an offer of a doctor's degree at the University of Aberdeen. Gray was genuinely flattered, but, in Johnson's laconic phrase, 'he thought it decent to refuse'. The reason for his refusal has some bearing on Gray's attitude to his own university:

I have been, S^r, for several years a Member of the University of Cambridge and formerly (when I had some thoughts of the profession) took a Batchelor of Laws degree there: since that time, though long qualified by my standing, I have always neglected to finish my course and claim my Doctor's degree. Judge therefore, whether it will not look like a slight and some sort of contempt, if I receive the same degree from a sister-university.

I certainly would avoid giving any offence to a set of Men, among whom I have pass'd so many easy and (I may say) happy hours of my life.

Clearly, there is feeling as well as formality in this letter and to Mason, in particular, Gray frequently wrote in a spirit of gaiety and in language which Matthew Arnold discreetly called Hogarthian, to welcome his beloved 'Scroddles' to the 'copuses and Welch rarebits' of Pembroke or to the coffee-house company which included Powell (Master of St John's), Marriott (Master of Trinity Hall) and Glynn, the physician, as well as Brown and Palgrave and Delaval from Pembroke.

Nor was Gray wholly indifferent to academic preferment. When the Regius Professorship of Modern History had fallen vacant in 1762, he allowed himself to be 'cocker'd and spirited up' by his friends, and his name went forward to Lord Bute. Nothing came of this except a polite reply and a promise of future service; but when in 1768 the vacancy recurred and Gray received an offer of the Chair through the Duke of Grafton, he was genuinely gratified especially by the Duke's remark that 'from private as well as public considerations, he took the warmest part in approving this measure of the King's'. It was, no doubt, through Stonhewer's influence that the offer was made and when Gray went to Court to kiss the King's hand, he was greatly flattered by the King's own remarks; 'but', he wrote, 'the day was so hot and the ceremony so embarrassing to me, that I hardly know what he said'.

When the Duke of Grafton was installed as Chancellor of the University in the following year, Gray felt that, much as he disliked writing to order, he must, as in private duty bound, offer to write the Installation Ode. So the *Odicle*, as he called it, was sent to the Vice-Chancellor in April, submitted to the Chancellor in June and then rehearsed again and again for musical performance.

The installation took place on 1 July and there were turbulent scenes at the Senate House. The doors were rushed and the Proctors endeavoured to clear the house of strangers. One lady lost both her shoes and another a diamond pin; Gray's Ode was described as being 'well set and performed, but charged with obscurity'. In the middle of July Gray left Cambridge for the vacation; he spent two months with Wharton at Old Park, Durham, and then made a tour through the Lake District, Lancashire and Yorkshire. Soon after his return to Cambridge his friend, Norton Nicholls, introduced to him Charles Victor de Bonstetten, a young Swiss to whose charm he succumbed with such completeness that after Bonstetten's departure in April 1770 he wrote: 'My life now is but a perpetual conversation with your shadow' and he was afflicted with a deeper sense of desolation than he had known for years. But a six months' ramble through Worcestershire, Gloucestershire, Monmouthshire, Herefordshire and Shropshire ('five of the best counties this Kingdom has to produce') cheered him in health and spirits and though the gout pinched him from time to time, he was prepared to say ''tis well, it is nothing worse', and by the end of October he was writing his customary gossip to Mason about the high tables of Pembroke and St John's.

Meanwhile, his conscience was stirred about his duties as Professor. He planned an inaugural lecture, in Latin, on an elaborate scale, but low spirits and bodily indisposition militated against its completion and, according to Mason, he contemplated resigning the Chair.

One Pembroke event, however, temporarily cheered him: Roger Long, the Master, died at the age of ninety on 16 December 1770 and five days later was buried in a vault of the College Chapel. This time there was no need for lobbying or intrigue on the part of Gray or anyone else. On the very day of the funeral James Brown was elected Master and Gray wrote gaily to Wharton telling him that the old Lodge had got rid of all its harpsichords and that its inhabitant was lost in it like a mouse in an old cheese.

But as the months went on, gout and depression grew worse. For a time Gray had contemplated a journey with Nicholls to Switzerland to see Bonstetten, but he got no farther than London and in May he wrote to Wharton 'Till this year I hardly knew what (mechanical) low-spirits were: but now I even tremble at an east-wind'. By the end of June the gout had left him, but a more serious disorder had shown itself. On 22 July 1771 he returned to Cambridge; dining in hall on the 24th he had a sudden fit of nausea and on the 30th he died in his rooms. James Brown was with him until half-an-hour before his death and on 17 August wrote to Wharton:

> Every thing is now dark and melancholy at Mr Gray's Room, not a trace of him remains here, it looks as if it had been for some time uninhabited and the room bespoke for another inhabitant.... The thoughts I have of him will last and will be useful to me the few years I can expect to live. He never spoke out, but I believe from some little expressions I now remember to have dropt from him for some time past he thought himself nearer his end than those about him apprehended it.

So ended Gray's life. It was not a life of normal happiness, but it would be wrong to think of Gray simply as a sensitive plant imperfectly nourished in an alien soil. It was of his own choice that he lived in Cambridge and it is doubtful whether he would have been happier, or as happy, anywhere else. His was the temperament that craved affection and intimacy, but was incapable of making the frank approach that evokes affectionate response; and the silence which was the manifestation of his own discomfort frequently militated against easy companionship. Thus, when in 1770 he for the first time met Richard Farmer (Master of Emmanuel and author of the *Essay on the Learning of Shakespeare*), there seemed to be a wide gulf between the two men: Farmer was hearty and downright and untidy; Gray was shy and fastidious and elegant. Then, fortunately, they met at dinner in Mr Oldham's rooms in Peterhouse. The ice was broken and a genuine friendship formed on the basis of a common interest in scholarship. After Gray's death, Farmer could but lament the shortness of their acquaintance. Charles Bonstetten, in his *Souvenirs*, naturally laid emphasis upon Gray's loneliness; but, as Mr Ketton-Cremer has remarked, his picture of the academic background is painted in over-sombre colours. The description of eighteenth-century Cambridge as a collection of monasteries inhabited by library-rats in human shape is clearly the rhetoric of a transient observer. On the other hand, his account of Gray's silences is convincing: 'To be reminded of his own poetry was hateful to him. He would never let me speak of it. When I quoted some of his own poems, he closed his mouth like a stubborn child.'

Here, as often, one is reminded of the Cambridge life of A. E. Housman—the solitary walks, the caustic comment, the rarity of poetic outburst, the reverence for scholarship, the accuracy of observation, the meticulous proof-correction, the silences. Yet to both of them Cambridge brought such happiness as they were capable of enjoying and both were grateful for it.

Despite his solitariness of spirit, Gray could, and did, enjoy conviviality. He took a malicious pleasure in satirising the scandalous and eccentric figures of the academic world, but he also took genuine and full-hearted pleasure in the society of his Cambridge friends. Many of the occupations he loved best—observation of birds and flowers, music, wide reading in ancient history—were most easily pursued in solitude; but to an evening party in college or a coffee-house he would summon his friends with unaffected gaiety. Travel he loved, since it enabled him to enlarge his observations of natural beauty and of ancient monuments; but he was always glad to return to Cambridge. There he could be solitary or sociable, as he chose; there, in a corner of the second court of Pembroke, was his home.

V. TWO CLERGYMEN

1. *JAMES BERESFORD*

ON Thursday, 3 June 1784, Johnson and Boswell climbed into the Oxford post coach at Bolt Court. In the coach were two other passengers—a Mrs Beresford and her daughter. Boswell describes them as 'very agreeable ladies' and Mrs Beresford, having read the way-bill, whispered to him: 'Is this the great Dr Johnson?' Still whispering, fortunately, she told Boswell that her husband had been a member of the American Congress. Warned to avoid that topic, the ladies were well content to listen to Johnson, and Johnson was in a mood for talking. He remarked, for instance, that he thought he was worth something more than a thousand pounds and that he proposed to leave Frank Barber an annuity of seventy pounds a year; he also commented on Miss Beresford's knotting: 'Next to mere idleness I think knotting is to be reckoned in the scale of insignificance.' But he was honest enough to add that he had once tried, without success, to learn the craft himself.

Miss Beresford was charmed. 'How he does talk!' she said to Boswell, 'Every sentence is an essay', and later she told her brother James, then an undergraduate at Oxford, that the engraving of Reynolds's portrait which was used as a frontispiece to the *Lives of the Poets* was the 'most correct likeness' she had seen.

James Beresford was born at Upham, in Hampshire in 1764. He went to Charterhouse (Mrs Bathurst's house) in 1773 and to Merton College, Oxford in 1781. He took his degree in 1786 and was elected to a fellowship in the following year. He remained a Fellow until 1812, when he was presented by his college to the living of Kibworth Beauchamp in Leicestershire and there he lived until his death in 1840. He was unmarried. Unlike some other country parsons, he left no diary and there is but scant material for biography. His bibliography, however, is more informative.

A man who had the good fortune to be elected a Fellow of his college in 1787 was not harassed by the spectre of research; he was not, on the other hand, compelled to be idle. He could sit back comfortably and make his choice of such literary pursuits as were congenial to him. Thus some of Beresford's earliest writing is to be found in *The Looker-On*, a periodical paper produced in Oxford in 1792, and largely written by William Roberts, who used the pen-name of the Reverend Simon Olivebranch. Roberts, who was later to become a prominent Evangelical, a hostile critic of Byron and an enthusiastic biographer of Hannah More, accepted contributions from other writers and among them was James Beresford. Boswell's *Life of Johnson*, published in the preceding year, was evidently in Beresford's mind and one of his pieces in *The Looker-On* was a Boswellian pastiche:

> We talked of public places; and one gentleman spoke warmly in praise of Sadler's Wells. Mr C—, who had been so unfortunate as to displease Dr Johnson and wished to reinstate himself in his good opinion, thought he could not do it more effectually than by decrying such light amusements as those of tumbling and rope-dancing; in particular he asserted that 'a rope-dancer was in his opinion the most despicable of human beings'. Johnson (awfully rolling himself as he prepared to

speak and bursting out into a thundering tone) 'Sir, you might as well say that St Paul was the most despicable of human beings. Let us beware how we petulantly and ignorantly traduce a character which puts all other characters to shame. Sir, a rope-dancer concenters in himself all the cardinal virtues.'

The spectacle of Johnson talking for victory is then presented at length and with considerable ingenuity, Boswell commenting at the end: 'How wonderfully does our friend extricate himself out of difficulties. He is like quicksilver: try to grasp him in your hand and he makes his escape between every finger.'

There have been many who have embarked upon Boswellian imitation; Beresford must have been one of the earliest and he is by no means the least effective. But Boswell was not his only target; he had also read Gibbon and in another paper in *The Looker-On* described the career of a light-fingered Irish adventurer:

The walls of Ranelagh were the scene of his maiden claims upon the involuntary contributions of the public; and in the transient revolution of a single evening a Knight of the Bath, nine Peers of the Realm, and five others of the brightest luminaries in the globe of fashion were reduced, by the fingers of the Son of Waldron, to the necessity of enquiring the hour of the night from those of their friends in whose fobs he had still left the sources of information.

An easier target was the Reverend James Hervey, the Methodist author of the extremely popular *Meditations and Contemplations* which reached its 25th edition in 1791. He was, in Beresford's view, a writer who 'could find a resemblance between religion and a radish, or draw the fire of devotion out of cucumbers; to whom every thorn was the thorn of Glastonbury and every bush contained a divinity; who could make up the ten commandments into a nosegay for the bosom and squeeze morality for a dozen pages out of a green gooseberry'. After which Beresford presents the reflections of such a writer upon a visit to Covent Garden Market:

> Even the low-born and grovelling potatoe might, on such an occasion, rise from its earthy habitation and, in a strain of native Hibernian eloquence, confound the boldest orator in the courts of Flora. And which could we select, among all these various tribes, as better entitled to the honourable privilege of pleading for the rest? For surely we shall not, like the wordling, measure desert by external standards; we shall not appreciate the pulp of the potatoe by the humility of the situation in which it grows, or under-rate the qualities of this precious plant because its retiring modesty renders it necessary to dig it from its courted obscurity.... And why does it sequester its plain, I had almost said clumsy form, from the sight of man, but for the noblest purposes, viz., that when our summer-friends of the garden have deserted us in our need, it may bring forth its stores in the winter adversity of our tables and endure, for the gratification of our capricious appetites, sometimes the ordeal of the gridiron, sometimes the martyrdom of the faggot, and sometimes the lingering and cruel persecution of the salamander.

Here Beresford was in good company. Johnson had a similarly low opinion of the writings of James Hervey. At the inn at Inveraray in 1773 he called for some books and the waiter brought him Hervey's *Meditations*. Scornfully, and for Boswell's benefit, he improvised a *Meditation on a Pudding*.

Beresford returned to Boswellian imitation in 1802, when he contributed a *Dialogue between Boswell and Johnson in the Shades* to William Mudford's *Critical Enquiry*. This was separately published, together with another dialogue between Handel and Braham (the famous tenor), in 1804. The Boswell-Johnson dialogue was based on the talk about the Cornish drink, Mahogany, at Sir Joshua Reynolds's dinner-party on 30 March 1781; but it is not one of the happiest of Beresford's *jeux d'esprit*.

Meanwhile, he had applied himself to a task more appropriate to an eighteenth-century Fellow of a college —a translation of the *Aeneid*. To this he turned in no dilettante spirit. In a leisurely but careful preface he explains his views on the proper function of the translator. In spite of his respect for Dryden as a great master of rhyme, he weighs 'the comparative advantages of rhyme and blank verse in Englishing the sublimer poets' and has no hesitation in 'assigning pre-eminence to the latter'.

> The Ancient Poets [he writes] have suffered as much from the luxuriancy as the poverty of the British ground into which they have been hitherto transplanted. It seems to have been wholly overlooked by the bulk of our Translators, that the great principle which should actuate them is a wish to extend and perpetuate their Author's renown; and this, as must be evident, can only be effected by the closest imitation which it is in their power to produce.

The proper function of a translator of poetry is still as controversial as it was 150 years ago. In Beresford's view, the sole business of a translator was to be a 'faithful Representer'. He did not expect all his readers to agree with him and his final paragraph is clearly reminiscent of a more famous Preface. 'No work', he quotes 'was ever yet spared out of tenderness to its author' and the last sentence is frankly Johnsonian: 'Prepared, therefore, as

I am to welcome success with gratitude, I am no less fortified to meet disappointment with submission.'

Certainly, Beresford's version exemplifies his adherence to fidelity rather than to poetic fire. It begins:

> Arms and the Man I sing, who first, Fate-driv'n
> From Ilium's coast, thence to Italia came
> And the Lavinian shore; wide-toss'd was he
> By stress of Pow'rs above on flood and field,
> Through fell Saturnia's memorable rage.

For the untranslatable *Sunt lacrimae rerum* he offers:

> Lo Priam here! behold here glory's praise
> Ev'n in these regions tears are found to flow
> And mortal mis'ries touch the feeling breast.

And for *Parce subiectis*...

> To rule o'er nations, Roman, be thy care;
> These be thine arts, to lay the laws of peace,
> To spare the vanquish'd, and bring down the proud.

Thus, while Dryden indulged what has been called 'the glorious rush of his poetic style', Beresford was content to deliver a 'Loeb' in blank verse. His list of subscribers was substantial, including eleven Fellows and one undergraduate of his college and the work was gracefully dedicated to his old headmaster, Samuel Berdmore, 'as an appropriate expression of acknowledgement for those instructions to which it owes its birth'.

Beresford's literary interests were not exclusively classical, for in 1796 he published *The Knights of the Swan, or the Court of Charlemagne* from the French of the Countess de Genlis. Evidently, he was not burdened with college administration. Merton College, during his period of residence, appointed three deans, three bursars and other minor officers. These offices were held by the Fellows in turn, but Beresford escaped all of them. No doubt he was happier in his literary experiments; in 1805 he produced *The Song of the Sun*, an imitation of the Edda, and a poem of the same year on the Battle of Trafalgar shows that he was not entirely detached from the contemporary scene.

Thus, in a little more than ten years Beresford's literary output was varied in character and considerable in quantity. Yet, if he had written no more after 1805, he would be completely forgotten. In fact, he is remembered, so far as he is remembered at all, for the work of which the first volume appeared, anonymously, in 1806 with the elaborate, but discouraging title: *The Miseries of Human Life; or the Groans of Timothy Testy, and Samuel Sensitive. With a few supplementary Sighs from Mrs Testy. In twelve dialogues.* The Preface is addressed 'To the Miserable', that is, to those children of misfortune who arrogate to themselves a kind of sovereignty in suffering. These are bidden to behold a Pageant of calamities which will call them to renounce their sad monopoly. The pageant is displayed in the form of dialogues in which Sensitive and Testy, after an introductory talk, pour out their woes to each other under various headings. The first is 'Miseries of the Country', such as:

Walking through a boundless field of fresh ploughed clay land; and carrying home, at each foot, an undesired sample of the soil of about 10 or 12 pounds weight.

Or

While walking with others, in a line, through a narrow path, being perpetually addressed by the lady immediately before you, who although she never turns her head in speaking, and a roaring wind from behind flies away with every soft syllable as it is uttered (like an eagle with a dove), seems to consider you as provokingly stupid for making her repeat her words twenty times over.

Or

On Christmas eve—being dunned by several parties of rural barbarians, on account of having stunned you by screaming and bellowing Christmas carols under your windows.

Next come the 'Miseries of Games and Sports'—and Tom Testy's comment on cricket is not without historical interest:

After a long and hard service of watching—bowled out at the first ball. Likewise, cricket on very sloppy ground, so that your hard ball presently becomes muddy, sappy and rotten—a jarring bat—a right hand bat for a left-hand player....

London provided some miseries which may still be experienced, such as:

In going out to dinner (already too late) your carriage delayed by a *jam* of coaches.

Or

The *meridian midnight* of a thick London fog—leaving you no method of distinguishing between the pavement and the middle of the street; much less between one street and another —the 'palpable obscure' pursuing you into your parlour and bed-chamber, till you can neither see, speak nor breathe.

From London there is a natural transition to the 'Miseries of Travelling':

In travelling on horse-back through an uninhabited country, enquiring your way, as you proceed, of different rustics, each of whom, besides giving you unintelligible directions as to your road, represents the place in question as many miles farther off than it had been reported by the last; thus making you seem to *recede* in your *progress*;—not to mention your expence of time and temper, from their anxious and *useful* enquiries as to the point from which you started, together with their rigmarole wonderings and lamentations at the number of miles which you have travelled out of your way.

The stage-coach also provides many miseries, such as:

On entering a stage-coach for a long journey, finding (amongst other pleasant inmates) at least one muddling mother, with a sick—but not silent—infant:—windows all as close as wax, for the poor child's sake!

Social life offers a wide range of examples:

On entering the room, to join an evening party composed of remarkably grave, strict and precise persons, suddenly finding out that you are drunk; and (what is still worse) that the company has *shared* with you in the discovery—though you thought you were, and fully intended to be, rigidly sober.

Or

After having left a company in which you have been galled by the raillery of some wag by profession—thinking, at your leisure, of a repartee which, if discharged at the proper moment, would have blown him to atoms.

Or

Paying a long visit at the retired house of a well-meaning soul, whose only idea of entertaining you is that of never leaving you a moment by yourself.

Dipping thus sporadically into Beresford's pages one may divide his comments, from the modern point of view, into two classes—those with an antiquarian, and those with a perennial, interest. Thus, among the 'Miseries of

Reading and Writing' an entry such as the following provokes reflection upon the changed conditions of letter-writing, as compared with 150 years ago:

> In writing—neither sand, blotting paper, nor a fire, to dry your paper, so that, though in violent haste, you sit with your hands before you, at the end of every other page, till the ink thinks proper to dry of itself;—or toiling your wrist for ten minutes together, with a sand-glass that throws out two or three damp grains at a time.

On the other hand, there is little difficulty in recognising this record of misery:

> Receiving, 'from the author', a book equally heavy in the literal and the figurative sense; accompanied with entreaties that you would candidly set down in writing your detailed opinions of it in all its parts.

'Miseries of the Table' are naturally plentiful and among them is one of the rare allusions to college life:

> In a college-hall—sitting at dinner on a bench nailed to the floor, and at such a distance from the table (nailed down also) that you feed in the position of a rower, just beginning his stroke.

Others are of more general application:

> Dropping in upon a friend at the dinner-hour, upon the strength of his *general* invitation and at once discovering, from the countenance and manner of his Lady, that you'd better have waited for a *particular* one.

From the table Beresford passes to 'Miseries Domestic'. Here is one illustrating the social graduations of the time:

> The harrowing necessity of asking a person to dine in your house, who is in that critical class of life which makes him not quite a proper guest at your own table, and at the same time, a few grades too high for that of the servants:—no second table.

Here, on the other hand, is a problem that is still with all of us:

> Cleansing the Augean stables;—or, in other words, undertaking the labour of digesting into its proper place each of a thousand different articles, of as many different uses, sorts and sizes (books—phials—papers—fiddles—mathematical instruments—drawings and knick-knacks without end) which have been for weeks or months accumulating upon the tables, chairs and shelves of your library, and which no servant is able to set to rights—so that you have been, yourself, obliged to await the tardy conjunction of activity and leisure, before you can enter upon the dreary drudgery of subduing them into arrangement.

The series concludes with groups of 'Miseries Personal' and 'Miseries Miscellaneous'. Of the former one example may be quoted:

> When in the gout—receiving the ruinous salutation of a muscular friend (a sea-captain) who, seizing your hand in the first transports of a sudden meeting, affectionately crumbles your chalky knuckles with the gripe of a grappling-iron; and then, further confirms his regard for you, by greeting your tenderest toe with the stamp of a charger.

With one of the 'Miseries Miscellaneous', resident members of an ancient university may feel a peculiar sympathy:

> Shewing the colleges, public buildings, and other remarkables of the University, for the 500th time, to a party who discover no signs of life during the whole perambulation.

Whatever one may think of *The Miseries of Human Life* today, it must be recognised, historically, as one of the best sellers of its time. Published in 1806, it reached its 8th edition in the following year, by which time Beresford felt encouraged to offer a second volume of miseries.

Originally the work had been published anonymously, but the author's name was inadvertently printed on the title-page of the 6th edition. At the end of the second volume, Beresford explains his motive:

In defence of this concealment, should a defence be required, he simply pleads his *Profession*; with the sacred character of which it might not have been considered as strictly accordant, to connect his name with a Publication so remarkably abounding in levities, until it should be as generally felt, and allowed, as he would fain presume it now to be, that those levities are sanctioned by his ulterior views. He confidently flatters himself that no reproach of such a nature as is here supposed can fairly fasten upon any attempt, however imbecile, to cool the blood of the petulant—to rebuke discontent erected upon fictitious grounds—to strengthen the guards of patience under evils of the meaner kinds and degrees—to substitute laughter, as the remedy of those evils, for violence or lamentation, which are, in reality, but their symptoms—to chastise the fopperies of preposterous delicacy and refinement—and as the main result of his undertaking, to establish in the heart that general temper of mildness, suavity and good humour, which is not merely a component part of general philanthropy, as well as of individual peace, but which (to extol it not more highly than it deserves) must be regarded as one of the main pillars of the Christian character.

Here Beresford is clearly conscious of the responsibilities of his cloth and his apologia was no doubt provoked by the remarkable popularity which his work achieved. No less a critic than Sir Walter Scott devoted twelve pages to it in *The Edinburgh Review* and described the humour of the book as typically English:

The Englishman feels the satisfaction of grumbling over his misfortunes to be, on many occasions, so much greater than the pain of enduring them, that he will beg, borrow, or steal, or even manufacture calamities, sooner than suffer under any unusual scarcity of discontent. He knows, indeed, that miseries are necessary to his happiness, and though perhaps not quite so pleasant at the moment as his other indispensable enjoyments, roast beef and beer, would, if taken away, leave just as great a craving in his appetites as would be occasioned by the privation of these national dainties.

Similarly, *The Eclectic Review* gave six pages of favourable comment on the book and noted with satisfaction that, although the volume was sprinkled throughout with facetious parodies, the phraseology of Scripture had not been prostituted to the purposes of wantonness. It also correctly identified the author as 'Mr Beresford who formerly published a highly respectable, but neglected, translation of Virgil'. On the other hand, *The Gentleman's Magazine* was mildly patronising:

It is written in the language of a gentleman and contains several well-applied classical quotations and puns. The collection, to say no more of it, is pleasant and harmless.

The Monthly Review hailed Beresford as a moral apothecary, but warned him that a good conceit may be worn threadbare.

Further evidence of the popularity of the *Miseries* is seen in the many imitations it provoked, such as *The Pleasures of Human Life* by Hilaris Benevolus and Co. and *The Comforts of Human Life* by Charles Chearful and Martin Merryfellow. Very different from these playful parodies was *An Antidote to the Miseries of Human Life in the History of the Widow Placid and her daughter Rachel* (1807), published anonymously by Harriet Corp. This *Antidote* was in no sense an imitation, but a serious comment from the point of view of a Quaker. 'I already perceive', says Mrs Placid, 'that the book is designed to burlesque the petty troubles of life and I wish the readers may so apply it, as to derive a good moral and be led from it to see the extreme folly of suffering their tempers to be injured by such ridiculous evils.' A reviewer of the *Antidote* remarked that, as a clergyman, Mr Beresford would probably not be sorry to find his frivolities seriously terminated—a conjectural probability that may well be doubted.

One further feature of the *Miseries* should be noted. The first edition contained a coloured frontispiece by W. H. Pyne, depicting Timothy Testy, Mrs Testy and Samuel Sensitive in attitudes of extreme misery. But Beresford was an amateur of the arts as well as of literature and the frontispiece of his second volume, as also of later editions of the first, is an engraving of a crusty and untidy figure uncomfortably seated on a high stool, holding in his left hand a teacup of which the contents are overflowing into his lap. The title is 'Miseries Personified' and the engraving is from a drawing by James Beresford. Further, at the end of the second volume there are 'Proposals for publishing by subscription a Print, in the Line manner and in half length designed as a Character of Falstaff from a Drawing by the Rev. James Beresford'. Whether sufficient subscribers were forthcoming is not recorded.

In 1809 The Rev. Thomas Frognall Dibdin, F.S.A., published *The Bibliomania or Book-Madness...in an Epistle addressed to Richard Heber, Esq.* In the course of this work he briefly surveyed the main symptoms of the disease, namely, a passion for Large Paper Copies, Uncut Copies, Illustrated Copies, Unique Copies, Vellum

Copies, First Editions, True Editions and Black Letter Editions. In a footnote he referred to *The Miseries of Human Life* as an 'ingenious and witty work'. Whether provoked or not by this reference, Beresford quickly seized upon Dibdin's work as an opportunity for satirical parody and in 1810 *Bibliosophia, or Book-Wisdom...by An Aspirant* appeared. The satire is applied with rather a heavy hand, but it is still entertaining to set the two books alongside each other. Here is Beresford's final shaft of irony:

> We may live to raise an offspring, who shall extend the conquests of the Collector over so wide a field, as, finally, not to leave the *Student* a book to study. At least, we may expect to see our Eaglets drive these mid-day Owls from out their Palaces of Science, back to their native element in those monastic dungeons, their College-Libraries. Thence they ought never to have ventured forth—and there may again pursue their *reading*, amidst their fellow-owls and owlish fellows—drowsing, side by side, over their studies, to the dismal clank of the chains, in which they hang their Authors.

Two years after the publication of *Bibliosophia* Beresford was presented to the Rectory of Kibworth Beauchamp and it is to be regretted that he left few records of, and no reflections upon, his life as a country parson. The sole fragment of characterisation is that recorded by the late Bishop Knox in his *Reminiscences of an Octogenarian*. Bishop Knox had held the same living from 1884 to 1891 and in referring to the *Miseries of Human Life* writes of his predecessor:

> Being a misogynist who vanished into the shrubbery at sight of a petticoat, whose maidservants turned their faces to the wall if they met him on the stairs, he had full experience of these Miseries.

DR JOHNSON AND OTHERS

There is much more that one would like to know about Beresford's personal qualities and habits; but at least there is no doubt about his politics. Like many other Rectors, he wrote a *Discourse* in memory of George III which was 'principally addressed to the middle classes of Englishmen'. His opposition to Catholic Emancipation was violent and uncompromising and to him the advocates of parliamentary reform were a 'Body of English Traitors' who proposed to extend the sacred power of choosing Senators to 'the lowest, most ignorant, and most profligate members of society'.

Finding little comfort in political crusading, Beresford returned to literature and in 1824 published *The Cross and the Crescent*, an heroic, metrical romance partially founded on Madame Cottin's *Mathilde*:

> When Time was full, that consecrated Town
> Which had, through Ages, groan'd in servitude
> To Pagan Domination fierce and rude—
> Jerusalem—regain'd her glorious crown:
> Thy hand, Godfredo! swept th' Invaders down—
> Again the Sarazen prevail'd.—Again
> Rous'd by the voice of Christian woe,
> Europe, for one collective blow
> Pours all her nations to the Syrian plain—
> Avenge, avenge my Children slain!
> Be Zion wrested from the Godless Foe!

and so on for 360 pages.

Beresford's tenure of the Rectory of Kibworth was not uneventful. One outstanding event was the collapse of the church spire and the 'awful event' was described by the Rector in a letter to *The Gentleman's Magazine* in 1825. Symptoms of decay had been discovered two years before. A builder had been called in and repairs begun, but 'fissures and bulgings' of an alarming character appeared and the tower was vainly propped with inclined beams.

Unacquainted as yet with the imminent danger [wrote Beresford] I immediately went to the church, entered at the chancel door, advanced toward the West end where the mischief was gathering, heard the noises before mentioned, suddenly retired by the same door, proceeded round the East end toward the North gate of the Churchyard and there found the different workmen, with a few other persons intensely watching the steeple, and, as they told me, every moment expecting its fall. I took my station among them and in less than a minute after several premonitory crashings, the whole fabric bowed from the summit over the base, paused for a few seconds, and then, as with one collective effort, came down in a thundering cataract of ruins. A thousand years could not efface the impression made upon my soul and my senses by the grand, the astounding catastrophe. Through the immediate and most merciful interposition of God's providence not a life was lost, not the slightest bodily injury sustained by a human being. Praise be to His Holy Name!

The problem of restoration was discussed at many parish committee meetings, and it was finally agreed to rebuild the tower, but not the spire. These meetings may well have provoked in the Rector some further reflections upon the miseries of human life.

2. *BENJAMIN WRIGGLESWORTH BEATSON*

AT the annual service of Commemoration of Benefactors in the chapel of Pembroke College it is recalled that in 1874 'Benjamin Wrigglesworth Beatson, President, bequeathed to the Library his books numbering some 5000 volumes and made the College his residuary Legatee. The College applied the Bequest, which amounted to more than £10,000, in part to the foundation of scholarships to bear the name of Beatson and in part to the Library Fund'.

Beatson came up to Pembroke with an exhibition from Merchant Taylors' in 1821 and was sixteenth Wrangler and sixth Classic in 1825; he was elected to a Fellowship in 1827 and held it until his death in 1874. He was ordained in 1828 and served as chaplain of the College for many years. His principal contribution to scholarship was his *Index Graecitatis Aeschyleae* (1830), followed by his *Index Graecitatis Sophocleae*, and he also published a number of school books on Greek Iambic Verse, on Latin Prose Composition and on Ancient History. His long period of residence in College covered part of the transition from 'unreformed Cambridge' to Cambridge as reformed by Royal Commissions. As a Junior Fellow he took part in the election of Gilbert Ainslie to the mastership in 1828; as President (i.e. Vice-Master) and Senior Fellow he presided over the election of John Power in 1870.

Among the 5000 volumes which he bequeathed to the Library were many of his own note-books as well as two diaries and a book containing copies of letters. The diaries are not exciting, but they throw some light on Merchant Taylors' and Pembroke as they were in the early decades of the nineteenth century.

The first diary covers two of his years (1817–19) at Merchant Taylors' and contains the customary *olla podrida* of a schoolboy journal. Thus on 20 May 1817:

7-11. Cic. in Catilin. iv. 78 lines...
1-2. Dined rump steak
2-4. Cic. pro Murena, the first piece. This afternoon Carey was accused of selling books for waste paper—immediately condemned and expelled

On 10 October (Probation Day):

6-6.30. Ate a twist—prepared pens and ink
6.30-8. Went to M.T. Put into Greek a Latin piece on the poetry of Homer for 1st hour...
9-10. Read Rasselas. Greek theme on Ἀἰεν ἀριστεύειν
11-12.30. Washing. Breakfast—played with Boats
12.30-2. Latin piece on position of the organs of sense to be put into English...
3-4. Verses in Carolettam perituram (which Bull put by mistake for parituram)...
4-5. Dined cold beef and currant dumpling

At the beginning of November he spent a few days at Leytonstone with his mother and his brother Anby and on 3 November:

9-10. Bought in the village greens, butter and apples—a woman gave Anby a turnep to frighten people with—forgot it
10-11. Wrote verses on Hope for Mother
11-1. Took a walk to Snaresbrook—good fun
1-2. 5 Oysters for 3^d—dinner beef and the oysters

On 6 November he records:

This morning Princess Charlotte died at 2½ o'clock

and goes on:

7.30-8. Sat in the kitchen on the washing machine

Later in the day he adds:

Name of Princess Charlotte pronounced 10,000 times today at least but again he returns to his normal form of entry:

7.15–9. Read Hebrew Bible—supper cold pork

By 1819 he was growing a little tired of Election Day at Merchant Taylors':

11 June. 8.30–10.30. Washing—reading Pindar. Father gave me 2/6^d...
10.30–11.45. Went on the water with Anby, 6^d each—walked up and down St Swithin's Lane
11.45–2.0. After waiting a long time the speeches took place. Cary despatched his very fluently ...did not stay to hear the things called Epigrams read...
2.0–3.0. Dinner, gooseberry pudding

From these few excerpts it will be seen that, like Parson Woodforde and other diarists, Beatson is frequently careful to note the day's menu.

On 11 June 1821 he was at Merchant Taylors' for the last time. After being examined by Dr Trollope, he heard that he had a scholarship at Pembroke of £45 per annum, and four days later he records:

9.30–4.30. Travelled to Cambridge in the Union—rode inside to Hoddesdon, outside from Hoddesdon to Royston, inside from Royston to Cambridge...biscuit and ale at Ware

4.30–7. Went to PEMBROKE HALL and saw Mr Ainslie, my future Tutor. He bid us come again at 7—dinner at Eagle—Salmon and lobster sauce—Lamb chops, Duckling & peas & gooseberry pie—sherry, port

Thus fortified he returned to College:

7.0–11.0 At Pembroke—examined by Mr Ainslie—John xi, 1–6 & Cicero pro Cluentio....Saw King's, Trinity, Catharine, S. Johns, Cl. Hall—returned. Slept in No. 10 at Eagle

On 25 October Beatson again mounted the Union coach

at the Four Swans in Bishopsgate Street and was set down at the Blue Boar. He had his cap and gown fitted at Mason's in Sidney Street and the next day he was unpacking his luggage in 'pleasant rooms' in Pembroke. On his first Sunday morning he attended the Commemoration of Benefactors in Great St Mary's and saw the Vice-Chancellor and Proctors; in the evening he noted that the men in the College chapel were 'very irreverent'. On 13 November he was matriculated in the Senate House ('Bull dogs 2s.') and on the same day he comments: 'Ainslie a surly man, says one thing and means another.' Like all undergraduates of all generations, he had a low opinion of the Hall dinner. Thus on 20 November he complains that the beef is 'like horseflesh' and on the following day:

Hall. Roasted mutton, very small piece, eked out with biscuit. Men conspired to eat no pies till meat be better

From the first Beatson was a reading, rather than a rowdy, man. On 25 January 1822 he complains that 'some of our rowing men came and made an awful noise at my door', but later he admits that 'the college was never better off for reading men'. Like all scholars of his time, he had to face both the Mathematical and the Classical Tripos and he seems to have turned without effort from Euclid to Livy, from Newton to Porson and from Infinite Series to Aeschylus. At the end of his first year he set his heart upon a fellowship and, in his early days he took a somewhat jaundiced view of his own college. He disliked Ainslie from the beginning, and during his second year he wrote long, rambling letters to his cousin Sophia Smyth, pouring out his adolescent troubles and comparing his prospects unfavourably with those of his cousin John Gibson at Corpus. On 28 October 1822 he wrote:

> John has now been some time up and is pretty well settled into a new course of life.... Benet is by no means so formidable a jail as Pembroke. There is no starvation—no Ainslie... there are handsome Gyps [i.e. bedmakers] and there is not the same hazard attending his success or failure as there is in mine... and I must have a fellowship or I am undone....

In fact, Gibson cannot have thought highly of his prospects at Corpus, since he migrated to Sidney in 1823 and Beatson goes on to admit that he cannot really complain of his Gyp, 'Mrs James being the handsomest in the college and really not shocking when she is in a good temper'.

At the end of his first year Beatson was a college prizeman and he was not without friends. Among them was John Haughton, an Irishman who 'liked a social glass'. With Haughton he used to take country walks and on 8 February 1823 he records:

> Frolic with 3 girls on Trumpington Road—Haughton went off with one—I might have done had I not loved Brenda.

Haughton became Secretary, and later President, of the Union and Beatson notes that 'the post of Secretary was no sinecure'.

Another friend was J. H. Pooley who was admitted to Pembroke in 1820, but migrated in the following year to St John's of which he later became a fellow. On 24 January 1824 Beatson spent a jovial Saturday evening, from 5.30 p.m. to 1 a.m., with him in St John's. His record of the evening is curiously laconic: 'Pooley of St J., Cooper of Pemb. Pooley drunk—Cooper a fierce reader.' For the Christmas of 1824 Beatson decided to stay in Cambridge. Having obtained an exeat from Ainslie, he dined at the Eagle on soles, fowls and tarts with grapes and Madeira. This was followed by a supper of mutton chops and for breakfast on Christmas Day there was roast beef and pigeon pie. Christmas dinner was taken with his brother Anby and others at the Red Lion at Royston and the party returned to Cambridge at 11.45. On New Year's Day 1825 Beatson attended the Foundress' Feast in Hall; his comment on the menu was terse: 'tough goose and plum pudding'.

On 21 January he was at the College gates early ('very terrified') to hear the results of the Mathematical Tripos. The first news was that he was in the fourth bracket of Wranglers, i.e. between twelfth and twenty-sixth, and later he was definitely placed sixteenth. He tipped the porter 2s. Three weeks later he was sixth in the Classical Tripos and was urged by Graham, one of the examiners, to enter for the Chancellor's Classical Medal. 'Graham and Platt [another examiner for the Tripos]', he notes, 'would have put me higher—Johnians always fight for Johnians.'

In the Medal examination he was third, but he had no difficulty in securing a number of pupils and on 27 November Ainslie sent for him and gave him welcome news of a prospective fellowship. He was bidden to call upon the Fellows and on the following day was very graciously received by the Master (Joseph Turner) and enjoined to 'mix with the Fellows and be in harmony'. But Beatson was not wholly jubilant; there was 'an accursed speech to make to them all' and 'to go into orders directly a *sine quâ non*'. On the 29th he was admitted to his fellowship in chapel, 'taking the oaths and shaking hands with the Fellows'.

On 28 February 1828 he was examined for ordination in Christ's College Combination Room. With him, for ordination as priest, was Woolley Spencer, of Christ's, an old schoolfellow who 'knew nothing at all about anything' and 'was a very great bore indeed'. The ordination was on 2 March:

At Christ's Chapel, being ordained—£2. 18. 6 in all—a serious affair—Letters of Ord^n—Spencer a bore in his joy as much as in his grief.

On 3 August, Joseph Turner died after a reign of forty-four years as Master—the longest in the history of the College. Beatson was in London at the time and makes no reference to the event until the 11th when he records 'a letter from Tasker and Stockwell about the vacant mastership'. The Fellows lost no time and on the 15th Beatson writes:

Day of election of Master—called on Ainslie...a prayer, a Latin hymn—Scrutators & scrutation—then Ego. Benj Beatson nomino Gilb. Ainslie in officium custodis hujus coll—Vice's book—install^n—Dinner, soles fillet veal, haunch mutton—ducks—plumb pudding....

Later Beatson went to a supper of poached eggs with a Mrs Fysh and had 'a very pleasant evening'.

On 10 October he records:

At Senate house twice for Ainslie's D.D.—at the College meeting appointed a chapel reader—£20 they say

and in the following May he was told that he

might take the classical lectures next year being 5 lectures per week at £60 for the three terms.

Meanwhile he had his private pupils and his Sophoclean index ('getting on well, but dull work'). Of his work as chaplain there is little account, but on 7 June 1829 he writes 'All day busy with preparations for the eucharist'. The diary proper ends in 1829, but right through to the year 1865 Beatson continued a kind of short-title catalogue of his daily activities. These single-line, or half-line, entries become increasingly difficult to decipher as the handwriting grows smaller and smaller. Occasionally, however, there is an entry with a familiar ring. Thus, on 7 December 1847: 'Long coll. meeting on guests at quincentenary' and when the dinner was held on 31 December he notes:

Quincent Celeb[n]. Met at Power's... Turtle, Turbot, Langue, Bœuf roti, Pheasant, Cream, Gelee royale.... Between Andrews and Fisher the banker. Ended at 11.

Such are a few fragmentary glimpses of college life in the early nineteenth century. The broad impression left is that of an awkward, but not fundamentally unsociable, man. It is clear that Beatson enjoyed the pleasures of the table and the company of his friends and in vacation he frequently went to the theatre or the opera in London. But it is not surprising that he was unsuccessful in his candidature for the headmastership of the City of London School in 1840 and it would seem that he was never a 'good Combination Room man'. There is but one reference to a game of bowls in the garden, and he always seems to have been glad to get away from the company of the Fellows and to seek his friends elsewhere.

His reputation as a classical scholar rests upon his concordances to Aeschylus and Sophocles, which earned for him a modest paragraph in the *Dictionary of National Biography*; in his college the great value of his benefaction both to the Library and to the Scholarship Fund is remembered with becoming gratitude.

VI. MAX BEERBOHM[1]

1

'IF we could all of us follow Mr H. G. Wells's good example, dismiss the present from our minds and fix our eyes steadfastly on the future, then we could share his wholesome contempt for the past. But we can't.'

So spoke Max in a broadcast of 1936 which he entitled 'A Small Boy seeing Giants'. In that, as in other broadcasts, he liked to describe himself as 'an interesting link with the past', and it may reasonably be assumed that many of his listeners shared his inability to rise to the futurism of H. G. Wells and preferred to look back. For my own part, if I were asked to name a year which evokes in me a wondering nostalgia, I would select the year 1894.

In that year, I was a small boy and had no opportunity of seeing literary giants; but now, as I contemplate them bibliographically, I can recognise their stature. In 1894, Swinburne, standing at the head of living poets, produced his *Astrophel*; in the same year John Davidson's *Ballads and Songs* and William Watson's *Odes* appeared; drama was represented by Pinero's *The Weaker Sex*, Wilde's *A Woman of no Importance* and Yeats's *Land of Heart's Desire*; amongst the novels were Meredith's *Lord Ormont and his Aminta*; and Gissing's *In the Year of Jubilee*; Hardy, too, was still a novelist and produced *Life's Little Ironies*; George Moore's *Esther Waters* provoked trouble with the circulating libraries; and for those who liked what George Moore scorned as the 'healthy school' of writers there was *Trilby* or *The Prisoner of Zenda* or *The*

[1] Giff Edmonds Memorial Lecture, Royal Society of Literature, 1957.

Diary of a Nobody or *The Memoirs of Sherlock Holmes*. It was a rich and varied harvest and into the middle of it the first number of *The Yellow Book* was plunged.

Max was in his last year at Merton. A meeting with Aubrey Beardsley led to an invitation to contribute an essay to the projected journal and Max's career as a satirist was begun. His *Defence of Cosmetics* was printed in the first number of *The Yellow Book* and he was soon to learn that satire is one of the dangerous trades.

For behold! [he had written] the Victorian era comes to its end and the day of *sancta simplicitas* is quite ended. The old signs are here and the portents to warn the seer of life that we are ripe for a new epoch of artifice. Are not men rattling the dice-box and ladies dipping their fingers in the rouge-pot?

But the sedate journals of the period were not amused. *The Times* described the first number of *The Yellow Book* as a 'combination of English rowdyism with French lubricity', though later it conceded that the second number was less impudent than the first.

'The first volume', wrote *The Athenaeum*, 'evidently aims at novelty and yet it is not unlike in appearance the annual volumes of *Chatterbox* and other periodicals for young people.... Mr Beerbohm's "Defence of Cosmetics" is silly... Mr Beardsley's portrait of Mrs Patrick Campbell is libellous.' Other critics were more violent and Max was at pains to explain in the second number of *The Yellow Book* that his essay 'in opinion so flippant, in style so wildly affected' was meant for a burlesque upon the 'precious' school. To later numbers he contributed further essays. Among them was a satire on the Aesthetes and the Mashers of 1880 ('Dados arose upon every wall, sunflowers and the feathers of peacocks curved in every corner, tea grew quite cold while the guests were praising the Willow Pattern of its cup'). The period fascinated him, but he concluded that an exhaustive account of it would need a far less brilliant pen than his and accordingly he resigned his claims to Professor Gardiner and the Bishop of Oxford. At the end of 1895 he wrote an essay 'Be it Cosiness' for another periodical, *The Pageant*. Surveying the distant past of his undergraduate days, he sought the quietism of a London suburb where he could see the laburnum flowering in the little front garden and be grateful to the retired military man next door for the loan of his copy of *The Times*. In short, he belonged to the Beardsley period and felt himself a trifle outmoded. Younger men, with fresher schemes, had pressed forward and he stood aside with no regret.

It was clearly appropriate that the scattered writings of so distinguished a veteran should be collected. The publisher of *The Yellow Book* was a willing collaborator and *The Works of Max Beerbohm, with a Bibliography by John Lane* appeared in 1896. Thus, compactly, between the scarlet covers of a tiny quarto was the corpus of Max's literary work enshrined. *Finis coronat opus*. In fact, it was but a beginning and, to a less ingenious mind, the definitive character of the *Works* might have raised difficulties in the entitlement of supplementary volumes. But the problem was easily, and economically, solved. A second volume (1899) was, quite accurately, entitled *More*; it was followed, at stately intervals, by *Yet Again* (1909) and by *And Even Now* (1920).

Of course, this is not the whole bibliographical story, but for the moment I wish to dwell upon the later 1890's and upon the Edvardian period which followed.

In the mind of a reader of today the particular qualities of a Beerbohm essay—the gentle irony, the verbal precision, the neologisms, the careful polish, the consistent urbanity—are so firmly established, that he tends to reflect only upon the almost oracular supremacy which Max, in his later years, achieved. It is not always remembered that for fourteen years (from 1896 to 1910) he was a working journalist. In fact, he began earlier. While he was still at Oxford, he was caricaturing club types and Oxford types for the *Strand Magazine* and in the summer of 1894 he interviewed C. B. Fry at Wadham for the *English Illustrated Magazine*. After recalling a conversation with a decadent friend who deplored the athletic movement of the time—'the growing school of young men who wear their hair short, smoke briar pipes, and ride about to football matches on bicycles'—Max describes how he called upon the great all-rounder on a Sunday morning. It was 11 a.m., but Mr Fry (as Max punctiliously calls him throughout) was for once not in training and had seized the opportunity of making a very late breakfast and of smoking a pipe after it. Max particularly noted that there were pipes all over the room.

For myself (*egomet*, as Max would say) I find a peculiar fascination in the scene—the cheerful *bonhomie* of the athlete and the professional skill with which Max plied his questions. One can almost hear him asking: 'Is it good fun, jumping? Do you enjoy it?'

The reply is prompt and convincing: 'Rather, it's the best fun in the world.... You seem just to give one spring up and then the air rushes past you in a hurricane and there you are again on your feet, safe and sound.'

'But sometimes with a broken record?'

Mr Fry's attitude towards picture-galleries was similar, it appeared, to Miss Zuleika Dobson's view of music: 'I am very fond of pictures', he said, 'but I don't know anything about them.... I don't really know why a picture is good or bad, only just whether I enjoy looking at it or not. I take a great interest in heaps of things that I know nothing about.'

'For instance?'

'Well, politics for one, and golf for another—especially golf.... I do think it's a fascinating game.'

'Have you any idea of taking it up seriously, as a change from cricket and football?'

'Good heavens, no! I only look on golf as a kind of glorified croquet.'

Then there is talk about compulsory games in Public Schools and Max concludes: 'When I got out into the great quadrangle, I could not but envy the young athlete, with his off-hand ways and transparent happiness, living in this beautiful college.... I felt altogether that I should like to be "Fry of Wadham" myself.'

There is, I am convinced, more of wistfulness than of irony in that conclusion and I am tempted to digress for a moment on the subject of cricket. Remote as the game was from Max's interest, its very distance seems to have lent a wondering enchantment to his view. Thus, in the series of *Words for Pictures* which he did for the *Saturday Review* was a comment on a wood-engraving by William Nicholson, entitled 'Cricket':

> Observe the batsman! Slogger is legible in every bulging curve of him and the fielders have been scattered beyond the sides of this wood-block. See how fiercely, yet freely, he grips the willow in his fat hands, how ogreishly he smiles between

his whiskers at the doomed ball which must even now be flying towards him! The wicket-keeper, humped down on outspread legs, is more like an arch than a human being.... We are apt to forget how great a place in the world's economy is filled by this strange pastime.

But when the spirit of this strange pastime threatened to influence the work of the actor, Max scented danger. Commenting on the production of *Henry V* by another Oxford athlete, F. R. Benson, he wrote:

Alertness, agility, grace, physical strength—all these good attributes are obvious in the mimes who were, last week, playing *Henry the Fifth* at the Lyceum. Every member of the cast seemed in tip-top condition—thoroughly 'fit'.... The fielding was excellent, and so was the batting. Speech after speech was sent spinning across the boundary, and one was constantly inclined to shout 'Well *played*, sir! Well played *indeed*'. As a branch of university cricket, the whole performance was, indeed, beyond praise. But, as a form of acting, it was not impressive....

This is from one of the 470 pieces of dramatic criticism written for the *Saturday Review*. The cream of these was skimmed by Max himself in two volumes entitled *Around Theatres* (1924). But was it? When, in May 1898, Max succeeded Bernard Shaw as dramatic critic, he insisted that while he had a genuine love of literature and some knowledge of its technicalities, he took neither emotional nor intellectual interest in the drama. He had, he said, accepted an absurd post which might spoil and exhaust the talent he might otherwise be exercising in literary art. It is, therefore, not surprising that Max interpreted his function in a liberal sense and that among the pieces which have not been reprinted there are enshrined many reflections which throw light on his outlook not only upon the drama, but on literature and on life.

In the exercise of the literary art he never lowered his standards. He was cursed, he said, with an acute literary conscience and he conceived that one of the duties of a writer was to seem to write with ease and delight.

What distinguishes literature from journalism [he wrote] is not vigour and sharpness of expression: it is beauty of expression. To a man who shall create literature language must not indeed be an end in itself: it must be a means, a noble and very dear means. The true artist must love the material in which he works.... If he be a writer, it will not be enough for him to have so expressed his meaning that nobody can miss it or forget it: his meaning must have been so expressed as to waken in himself a pious joy in those harmonies of words and cadences which can be found if they are sought for.

At the same time, he dismissed with scorn the notion of the artist's self-sufficiency:

No artist does write merely for his own pleasure. Man is a gregarious animal and the artist himself is, despite all that has been said to the contrary, more or less human.... You may be sure that if you took the most intense and single-hearted artist in literature that ever lived and set him down, with pens, ink and paper on a desert island, he would produce little or nothing unless he had some reason to believe that he would ultimately be rescued; and be sure that if you came to rescue him, and if he had not been idle, he would meet you with his manuscript and would immediately read it to you on the beach.

Written in a decade which is commonly associated with the theory of 'Art for Art's sake', how salutary is the sheer common sense of such a paragraph. Furthermore, for all his pious search for harmonies of words and cadences, Max was sensitive to the dangers of the cult of the *mot juste* and a consideration of the dramatic version of *The*

Prisoner of Zenda led him to a comparison of Robert Louis Stevenson and Anthony Hope which is as refreshing as it is unexpected:

> Stevenson was always whittling and filing, embroidering and confectioning. He was always preoccupied with words... Mr Hope's invention of stories may be inferior to his, but Mr Hope has this vast advantage, that no reader can but be obsessed by Stevenson.... For my own part, I am quite happy to sacrifice a story for style. I rate the essayist far higher than the romancer.... But I cannot persuade myself to admit that Mr Hope's romances, as written by him, are not superior to Stevenson's. If this is a heresy, so much the better. It is only through heresies that criticism can progress.

Evidently *The Prisoner of Zenda* had a particular interest for Max, for when it was revived it led him to reflect upon the true criteria of dramatic excellence. Did the play offer a criticism of life as we know it? Did it create illusion in the playgoer? The answer is clear: 'Mr Hope's manner of making his play was not as of a man asking us to believe the story, but as of one inviting us to agree with him how delightful it would be if such things *could* happen. His play was, in the direct sense, a criticism of life. Its great point was in being so frank a fantasy.'

This reference to fantasy is peculiarly relevant to one part of Max's own work and to this I shall shortly return. Meanwhile it may be noted that the dramatic illusion he demanded must be one of two kinds: either the play should make him feel that he was listening to men and women whose problems and sufferings and gaieties were a part of actual life; or it should transport him to some realm of fancy in which he could willingly be absorbed while the curtain was up. Only rarely did the playwrights of the period satisfy one or other of these conditions. There were certain plays that he hated and he was not afraid to say so—*The Light that Failed,* for instance, or *The Passing of the Third Floor Back.* Sometimes he was captivated by the constructive skill of the playwright. Thus he wrote of Pinero's *His House in Order*: 'I cannot ignore the play's fundamental weaknesses. But I do not forget that my inferior self enjoyed the play immensely. Judged on a low plane, *His House in Order* takes very high rank indeed.'

Here the acute critical conscience is at work. It was not enough that a play should, in the modern phrase, be just 'good theatre'.

When Max looked back on his long period of apprenticeship on the *Saturday Review,* he was astonished at his own proliferation: 'On and on I went doggedly from the age of 25 to the age of 37. It seems incredible; but it is a fact', and he adds, without false pride or false modesty, that he never scamped his work. Like Samuel Johnson and some others before him, he might find the weekly demand irksome, but that was no excuse for the blunting of the literary conscience. Bernard Shaw once remarked, characteristically, that nothing that is not journalism will live as literature; Max might well have retorted that nothing that is not literature will live as journalism.

2

The *Saturday Review* was not the only journal for which Max wrote. When in 1909 he selected the material for *And Yet Again,* he had no notion, he said, that he had put his eggs into so many baskets—and by this time there were different kinds of eggs and different kinds of baskets. His first book of caricatures, *Caricatures of Twenty-five Gentlemen* (1896) was followed by *The Poets' Corner* (1904) and *A Book of Caricatures* (1907). Here I am concerned with the writings of Max Beerbohm, but I do not forget what Bohun Lynch wrote in 1921:

> The caricatures and the writings are not manifestations of two arts but of one. There are a number of proverbs...about shoe-makers sticking to their lasts and Jacks-of-all-Trades being masters of none. But these do not apply to Max Beerbohm who has but one trade. He is a satirist.

One of the most natural media of a satirist is that of parody, and the parodies collected in *A Christmas Garland* (1912) may, perhaps, provide the closest analogue to the caricatures. Yet the analogy may not be very close. Open one of the books of caricature, say, at a representation of Arthur Balfour. The immediate impression may well be one of grotesque absurdity—a prodigiously tall, slim figure surmounted by a tiny head. Max has seized upon the long frock-coat which dominated Balfour's appearance and exaggerated it to the highest point. The caricature of H. G. Wells in the same volume shows a reverse of the treatment. Wells's figure was short and undistinguished, with a brain bursting with futurist ideas; accordingly he is portrayed with a massive head and a stunted, insignificant body. In his face is all the earnest melancholy of the Utopian prophet.

From these two portraits one may suitably turn to the parody of Wells in *A Christmas Garland*. In the opening paragraphs of chapter xx of *Perkins and Mankind* there is little or no exaggeration. Much of it is so faithful to the original that although there is much to amuse there is nothing to shock or startle:

> The enormous house was almost full. There must have been upwards of fifty people sitting down to every meal. Many of these were members of the family....For the rest there were the usual lot from the Front Benches and the Embassies. Evesham was there, clutching at the lapels of his coat; and the Prescotts—he with his massive mask of a face, and she with her quick hawk-like ways, talking about two things at a time; old Tommy Strickland, with his monocle and his dropped g's, telling you what he had once said to Mr Disraeli; Boubou Seaforth and his American wife; John Pirram, ardent and elegant, spouting old French lyrics; and a score of others.

That might well be a paragraph taken straight from *The New Machiavelli*. But the satirist shortly appears—and the subject is Arthur Balfour:

> True there was Evesham. He had shown an exquisitely open mind about the whole thing. He had at once grasped the underlying principles, thrown out some amazingly luminous suggestions. Oh yes, Evesham was a statesman, right enough. But had even he ever really *believed* in the idea of a Provisional Government of England by the Female Foundlings?

It is the same with many of the other pieces in *A Christmas Garland*. The parody is the work of the same satirist, but the material requires different treatment. In the portrait the dominating characteristic is conveyed in a flash. As Raven Hill said: 'If Max sees a little man with nothing particularly strange about him except a big moustache, he goes for that big moustache.' Similarly, Max goes for Arthur Benson's sentimentality, for Arnold Bennett's provincialism, or for Chesterton's paradox; but he goes more quietly, opening with gentle pastiche and only gradually exposing the idiosyncrasies of the writer.

Occasionally he would employ what he called his 'habit of aping' in the spirit of an imaginary conversation and there is no better example of his astonishing capacity for imitation and adaptation than the poem which he entitled *A Luncheon*. In 1923 the then Prince of Wales lunched with Thomas Hardy on his way to visit the estates in his Duchy of Cornwall. It is not difficult to imagine how the scene would appeal to Max's percipient mimicry. On the one hand was the veteran poet and novelist:

> (Intensive vision has this Mr Hardy
>   With a dark skill in weaving word-patterns).

On the other hand was the young prince whose career Max had followed from the perambulator onwards:

> Lift latch, step in, be welcome, Sir,
> Albeit to see you I'm unglad
> And your face is fraught with a deathly shyness
> Bleaching what pink it may have had.
> Come in, come in, Your Royal Highness.
>
> Beautiful weather?—Sir, that's true,
> Though the farmers are casting rueful looks
> At tilth's and pasture's dearth of spryness.—
> Yes, Sir, I've written several books.—
> A little more chicken, Your Royal Highness?
>
> Lift latch, step out, your car is there,
> To bear you hence from this antient vale.
> We are both of us aged by our strange brief nighness,
> But each of us lives to tell the tale.
> Farewell, farewell, Your Royal Highness.

Such a piece, as Johnson said of Gray's *Elegy*, it is useless to praise. But I remember with pleasure that when I once told Max how highly I rated this poem, he replied 'Yes, that was a good one'. It was the considered verdict of an acute and detached critic.

Some of Max's best known and best loved satire is contained in *Seven Men*. Enoch Soames and Savonarola Brown are both ridiculous, but they are both infinitely pathetic. Max wants you to laugh at them, but he also wants you to be sorry for them. It is otherwise with T. Fenning Dodworth; there he is exposing a humbug and the satire is persistent and merciless:

> There was an old-established daily newspaper whose proprietor had just died.... Dodworth was installed in the editorial chair, gave the keynote to the staff, and wrote every night a leading article with his own incisive pen.... To uneducated readers the almost-daily-recurring phrase *Quos deus vult* had no meaning. Half-educated readers thought it meant 'The Lord watch between thee and me when we are absent one from another'. The circulation fell by leaps and bounds... Within six months that old-established newspaper ceased utterly to be. 'This' I thought 'really *is* a set-back for Dodworth'. I was far from right. The set-back was rather for myself. I received no payment for three or four of the book-reviews that I had contributed, and I paid two guineas for my share of the dinner offered to Dodworth at the Savoy Hotel.

Irony was inherent in Max's writing, but in the period following the First World War a mellow benevolence replaces the deliberately impish arrogance of the 1890's. Consider, for instance, the essay entitled *Hosts and Guests*. Light and cheerful in treatment, it is derived from an acute and accurate perception of the varieties of social experience: 'You ask me to dine with you in a restaurant, I say I shall be delighted. You order the meal, I praise it, you pay for it, I have the pleasant sensation of not paying for it.' What could be simpler or more fundamental than this candid dichotomy? And how characteristic is Max's own apologia at the end of the essay:

> I will not claim to have been a perfect guest.... I was a good one but.... I was rather *too* quiet, and I did sometimes contradict. And, though I always liked to be invited anywhere, I very often preferred to stay at home. If anyone hereafter shall form a collection of the notes written by me in reply to invitations, I am afraid he will gradually suppose me to have been...a great invalid, and a great traveller.

By the disruptions of war and the social changes which they accelerated Max was profoundly saddened, as when, lingering by the Golden Drugget he paused 'to bathe in the light that is as the span of our human life, granted between one great darkness and another'. Sadness of a more intimate kind is the theme of *William and Mary*. Except for some light chaff of William in his undergraduate days, there is no satire; its place is taken by a restrained but profoundly sympathetic picture of human happiness and human tragedy—*simplex tristitiis*. Sympathy, of a retrospective kind, is also the keynote of *A Clergyman*, that superb reconstruction of a Boswellian scene in which Max immortalises a cleric whose name even Boswell did not trouble to record:

> Fragmentary, pale, momentary; almost nothing; glimpsed and gone...he forever haunts my memory and solicits my weak imagination. Nothing is told of him but that once, abruptly, he asked a question, and received an answer.

And having told the story of that question and answer, Max concludes:

> 'A Clergyman' never held up his head or smiled again after the brief encounter....He sank into a rapid decline. Before

the next blossoming of Thrale Hall's almond trees he was no more. I like to think that he died forgiving Dr Johnson.

Coming from a writer of 'weak imagination', it is a notable essay.

What, in fact, was the quality of Max's imagination? Here I recall his dramatic criteria—either convincing presentation of actuality or convincing transference to a world of fantasy. To the world of fantasy he could be easily drawn; he commended *The Prisoner of Zenda* for being frankly a fantasy, a story which made people feel not that it was credible but 'how delightful it would be if such things *could* happen'. But is this, in fact, true of the multitude of common readers who have been captivated by Anthony Hope's romance? There is nothing magical or miraculous at the bottom of Rudolf Rassendyll's adventure. The theme, as Anthony Hope said himself, is the ancient one of mistaken identity with royalty and red hair thrown in; and the common reader found no difficulty in believing in the close likeness between two distant kinsmen. But when Max turned from essays and parodies to the creation of a story of his own, he went further. Free of the shackles of credibility, he could wander into fairy-land and, in *The Happy Hypocrite*, could endow Lord George Hell's mask with the power of transforming the insolent and purple face of a Regency buck into that of a virtuous lover. Here, indeed, is a story that is 'frankly a fantasy', but it is something very different from *The Prisoner of Zenda*.

For the scene of his most famous fantasy Max wandered not into fairy-land, but into Oxford—which for him, perhaps, was the same thing.

The story was begun while he was still in London,

writing for the *Saturday Review*, but laid aside. In a letter to Will Rothenstein in the autumn of 1911 he wrote:

> Zuleika will be with you anon. The proofs are flowing in, and the book will be out not later, I hope, than the first week in October. I am really very glad I found it impossible to go on writing the book in London years ago. I have developed since then; and the book wouldn't have had the quality it has now. It really is rather a beautiful piece of work—though it may be a dead failure in point of 'sales'—and on the other hand might sell quite well: just a toss up... If the binders and paper-makers don't play me false, the book will *look* nice; not like a beastly *novel*, more like a book of essays, self-respecting and sober and ample.

'More like a book of essays'—one recalls his earlier remark that he rated the essayist far higher than the romancer. Yet the subject demanded something more than a series of orderly essays. 'Oxford!' he wrote, 'The very sight of the word printed, or sound of it spoken, is fraught for me with most actual magic.' So there must be a story (Oh dear, yes, a story, as Mr Forster would say) and the story must not be trammelled by conventional probabilities; the magic must be allowed to work.

In a note to a new edition of the book in 1946 Max wrote: 'I myself had supposed it was just a fantasy; and, as such, I think, it should be regarded by others'; and those who enjoy fantasy for its own sake may well be happily carried along by the narrative as the pearls change colour and the Tankerton owls hoot and the Duke parades in the Meadows in his Garter robes and the undergraduates hurl themselves into the river for love of Zuleika. Less imaginative readers may, perhaps, grow a little weary of the ebb and flow of adoration and abuse between Zuleika and the Duke and of the Duke's meditations on the eternal verities; they prefer to re-read the descriptions of the many facets of the character of the heroine—the character, that is, not of Miss Dobson, but of Alma Mater Oxoniensis. What, for instance, is more Oxonian than that line of Roman Emperors who are commemorated in the first chapter of the book?

> Here in Oxford, exposed eternally and inexorably to heat and frost, to the four winds that lash them and the rains that wear them away, they are expiating, in effigy, the abominations of their pride and cruelty and lust. Who were lechers, they are without bodies; who were tyrants, they are crowned never but with crowns of snow; who made themselves even with the gods, they are by American visitors frequently mistaken for the Twelve Apostles.

There follows the brilliant sketch, in three pages, of the history of Judas College and, more intimately, the musings of a Merton man in the meadows:

> There lay Oxford far beneath me, like a map in grey and black and silver. All that I had known only as great single things I saw now outspread in apposition and tiny; tiny symbols, as it were, of themselves, greatly symbolising their oneness. There they lay, these multitudinous and disparate quadrangles, all their rivalries merged in the making of a great catholic pattern.... But if a man carry his sense of proportion far enough, lo! he is back at the point from which he started. He knows that eternity, as conceived by him, is but an instant in eternity, and infinity but a speck in infinity. How should they belittle the things near to him?... Oxford was venerable and magical, after all, and enduring.

Max's criticism of Stevenson as a novelist is surely applicable in some measure to himself, for the reader of *Zuleika Dobson* is obsessed not by Miss Dobson, but by

Max. Does not Zuleika confess that the literary flavour of her talk was an unfortunate trick she had caught from a writer, a Mr Beerbohm, who had once sat next to her at dinner somewhere? In short, we read *Zuleika Dobson* as Johnson read the novels of Samuel Richardson, not for the story, but for the sentiment—and the satire.

This somewhat lukewarm appreciation of the fantasy on my part may indeed seem ungracious, since I owe the friendship which I was fortunate to enjoy with Max for the last twelve years of his life entirely to the last page of *Zuleika Dobson*. For years that final, imperious demand for a special train to Cambridge had worried me. Was the journey accomplished? I was not prepared to accept Mr Forster's unsupported theory that the train was deflected into a siding at Bletchley. But if it did, in fact, reach its journey's end, into what maze of Cantabrigian fantasy did it lead? To nothing more serious, I conjectured, than to a special meeting of the Proctorial Syndicate. It was a proud and happy moment for me when Max told me that I had convinced him.

3

In a volume of caricatures published in 1923 and entitled *Things New and Old* Max depicted himself drawing at a small desk outside his Villino. He has long white hair and an even longer white beard; he wears a small skull cap and clumsy carpet slippers. Three caricaturists of the younger generation are looking down on him and 'wondering how long the veteran exile will go doddering on'.

But Max never doddered. It is true that he gave up drawing in his later years because he found himself producing photographic likenesses and in photographic drawing he was not interested.[1] But, at intervals, he continued to write and at the end of 1935, when he was temporarily living in London, some far-sighted genius induced him to come to the microphone. It was the beginning of the Indian summer of an essayist. Lecturing and public speaking had never been among Max's *parerga* and, with the instinctive percipience of the artist, he realised at once that broadcasting did not mean reading an essay aloud; in fact, he was driven to invent a new word for his essays—'Narrowcasts'. As he wrote in a prefatory note to a collection of his broadcasts, the pieces were composed for the ears of listeners and he trusted the inflexions of his voice to carry the finer shades of meaning and expression. It was a trust well placed. Thousands who had never heard of *The Yellow Book* or of the Duke of Dorset or of Savonarola Brown were enchanted by the precision, the humour, and the intimacy of the voice which told them what London had looked like forty years before; and for his friends it was like listening to him from the other side of the fireplace.

Two more broadcasts were delivered in 1936 and three more during the war years. 'Music Halls of my Youth', spoken in his 70th year, was remarkable in many ways and particularly in the way in which he entered into the spirit of his subject. Who that heard it can forget the beginning: 'Ladies and Gentlemen, or if you prefer that mode of address, G'deevning'? And when he went on to describe the songs of the Great MacDermott, the artist in him compelled him to give the music as well as the words. He couldn't sing, he said, but he gave what he called a croaking suggestion.

[1] But the abandonment was not complete. His last drawing (of George Moore) was done in January 1956, four months before his death.

Meanwhile, many honours had come to him—knighthood, honorary doctorates, an honorary fellowship of his college. On such things Max had poured plenty of youthful scorn; but, as he wisely said: 'After thirty one should quarrel with no man.' One of his rare public lectures was given at Cambridge in 1943—the Rede Lecture on Lytton Strachey. It was rehearsed with scrupulous care and beautifully spoken. His sympathetic treatment of Strachey led him to make some characteristic remarks on the art of writing:

> A true gift for writing...is not widely bestowed. Nor is a true gift for painting, or for playing the violin; and of that we are somehow aware. We do not say to a violinist 'Just think out clearly what you want to express and then go straight ahead. Never mind how you handle your bow', nor to a painter 'Got your subject and your scheme of colour in your head all right, eh? Then don't bother about how you lay your paints on, dear old boy.' Let us not make similar remarks to writers.

And then he returns to his old theme (*tamen usque recurret*) of the verbal preciosity which spoilt Stevenson as a novelist. But perhaps the most sympathetic reference was to Strachey's quotation of Talleyrand's remark that only those who had lived in France before the Revolution had really experienced *la douceur de vivre*. That was precisely what Max felt about pre-1914 England. Nevertheless, when the end of the Second War enabled him to return to Rapallo, life still retained a measure of sweetness for him. From time to time he was heard again on the air recalling memories of George Moore, or H. B. Irving, or William Morris, and presenting to his listeners a quiet, but intensely vivid picture of their idiosyncrasies. At luncheon on his 80th birthday (not in

Rapallo, but in a small inn on the top of the mountain behind the town) he received many tributes which pleased and amused him: there was a sheaf of congratulatory telegrams which included Sir Winston Churchill's; there was a Penguin edition of *Zuleika Dobson* published for the occasion; there was a bound volume of tributes from his friends; and there was a gigantic and incongruous sheaf of gladioli (fashionably enclosed in cellophane) presented by the very small son of the innkeeper. In the lovely Italian sunshine Max was smiling and content. Three years later, though physically frail, he was still happy to welcome an old friend at the Villino and to talk about old times and modern trends.

On my last visit to him, about six months before his death, I happened to show him a proof-copy of a volume of memoirs by an old contributor to *The Yellow Book*. As I expected, he was interested in some passages relating to Edward VII. What I did not expect was his quick perception and correction of a serious mistake in dates which had escaped the proof-reader.

Qualis artifex periit—but I prefer to recall his own dying words and to thank him for everything.